MW00861664

BUILDING A BETTER CHICAGO

LATINA/O SOCIOLOGY SERIES
General Editors: Pierrette Hondagneu-Sotelo and Victor M. Rios

Family Secrets: Stories of Incest and Sexual Violence in Mexico
Gloria González-López

Deported: Immigrant Policing, Disposable Labor, and Global Capitalism
Tanya Maria Golash-Boza

From Deportation to Prison: The Politics of Immigration Enforcement in Post–Civil Rights America
Patrisia Macías-Rojas

Latina Teachers: Creating Careers and Guarding Culture
Glenda M. Flores

Citizens but Not Americans: Race and Belonging among Latino Millennials
Nilda Flores-González

Immigrants Under Threat: Risk and Resistance in Deportation Nation
Greg Prieto

Kids at Work: Latinx Families Selling Food on the Streets of Los Angeles
Emir Estrada

Organizing While Undocumented: Immigrant Youth's Political Activism Under the Law
Kevin Escudero

Front of the House, Back of the House: Race and Inequality in the Lives of Restaurant Workers
Eli Revelle Yano Wilson

Building a Better Chicago: Race and Community Resistance to Urban Redevelopment
Teresa Irene Gonzales

Building a Better Chicago

Race and Community Resistance to
Urban Redevelopment

Teresa Irene Gonzales

NEW YORK UNIVERSITY PRESS
New York

NEW YORK UNIVERSITY PRESS
New York
www.nyupress.org

References to Internet websites (URLs) were accurate at the time of writing. Neither the author nor New York University Press is responsible for URLs that may have expired or changed since the manuscript was prepared.

Library of Congress Cataloging-in-Publication Data
Names: Gonzales, Teresa Irene, author.
Title: Building a better Chicago : race and community resistance to urban redevelopment / Teresa Irene Gonzales.
Description: New York : New York University Press, [2021] | Series: Latina/o sociology | Includes bibliographical references and index.
Identifiers: LCCN 2020035763 (print) | LCCN 2020035764 (ebook) | ISBN 9781479839759 (cloth) | ISBN 9781479814886 (paperback) | ISBN 9781479872282 (ebook other) | ISBN 9781479813568 (ebook)
Subjects: LCSH: City planning—Illinois—Chicago. | Urban renewal—Illinois—Chicago. | Social change—Illinois—Chicago.
Classification: LCC HT168.C5 G66 2021 (print) | LCC HT168.C5 (ebook) | DDC 307.3/4160977311—dc23
LC record available at https://lccn.loc.gov/2020035763
LC ebook record available at https://lccn.loc.gov/2020035764

A version of Chapter 3 was published in the *Journal of Urban Affairs*. See Gonzales, T. (2017). Two sides of the same coin: The New Communities' Program, grassroots organizations, and leadership development within two Chicago neighborhoods. *Journal of Urban Affairs*, 39(8), 1138–1154. Used with permission.

New York University Press books are printed on acid-free paper, and their binding materials are chosen for strength and durability. We strive to use environmentally responsible suppliers and materials to the greatest extent possible in publishing our books.

Manufactured in the United States of America

10 9 8 7 6 5 4 3 2 1

Also available as an ebook

For Grandma Pura, Granny Ruby, Mommy, Daddy, Ricky,
Mario, and Angela

For Pixel and Lucy
and
For Wilson

CONTENTS

FIGURES AND TABLES

Introduction

"This Is Why We Can't Have Nice Things"

I tell my students, "When you get these jobs that you have
been so brilliantly trained for, just remember that your real
job is that if you are free, you need to free somebody else. If
you have some power, then your job is to empower somebody else. This is not just a grab-bag candy game."
—Toni Morrison, "The Truest Eye"

Books saved my sanity; knowledge opened the locked places
in me and taught me first how to survive and then how to
soar.
—Gloria Anzaldúa, *Borderlands / La Frontera*

As a third-generation, multiracial, multiethnic Mexican American
from a low-income background, I had not planned on becoming a professor.[1] Such a future was far removed from anything I could imagine
as a high school student. I had not even planned on attending college. I
was not a model student—I skipped almost half of my senior year and
just barely graduated. I hated school, I hated being poor, and I hated
people's assumptions about me as a young Mexicana from the Pilsen
neighborhood of Chicago. Students like me—especially those who were
poor and Black, Mexican, or Puerto Rican—were disproportionately
penalized by teachers and administrators.[2] Everything from the way
we dressed and spoke to the questions we asked were grounds for dis-
ciplinary action. The curriculum did not reflect our realities, and we
were expected to follow authority blindly. Given these experiences, at
first I avoided college, which I imagined would be an extension of high
school. I chose instead to work several jobs in the formal and informal
sectors to help provide for myself and assist my family. This work took

me to various parts of Chicago, from the affluent, pristine neighborhoods of the lakefront to the working-class and poor communities of the West and South sides. Navigating these spaces and seeing how a city is planned politically, economically, socially, and racially planted the early seeds of my interest in uneven urban redevelopment. I also witnessed various ways that residents, including those in my own community, collectively worked to improve their environs and disrupt negative narratives of their neighborhoods. This interest eventually propelled me into my undergraduate and graduate studies and then into my academic career.

I share this context not to tell a story of overcoming odds—people from disenfranchised communities rarely "pick themselves up by the bootstraps." As sociologist Victor Rios highlights, it is extremely difficult to fulfill this American Dream narrative when you don't have any boots, let alone bootstraps, by which to pick yourself up.[3] Instead, I briefly outline my background to articulate two commonalities shared by Black, Puerto Rican, and Mexican American populations in the United States. The first, apparent to me and my friends at a young age, is the experience of inequality, as institutions treat racialized populations as inferior, insufficient, or unsatisfactory. Of course the experiences of people of color are far from homogenous. Puerto Ricans, African Americans, and Mexican Americans have unique histories of state violence, land dispossession, and political and economic repression rooted in racism, colorism, colonialism, slavery and servitude, and subordinate or nonexistent citizenship. Nevertheless, these populations share related and persistent experiences of discrimination and inequality. The second commonality is the impact of interlocking social structures that exacerbate their marginalization and that of all those who are poor or oppressed.

For residents, these interlocking structures are most evident at the neighborhood level. The way a neighborhood is envisioned, planned, and resourced directly impacts the life chances and presence of assets for local residents. A community with mostly one- and two-story homes, well-maintained and clean public spaces and local parks, a library, quality public schools, and a small business district has a very different feel from a neighborhood with mostly tenement housing, abandoned and vacant lots, garbage-strewn streets, and no areas for public leisure. Which neighborhood would you want to live in or walk through? Yet development decisions made at the municipal level limit many Black and Latina/o/x residents from accessing safe, clean, and healthy neighborhoods.[4]

These commonalities became ever more apparent as new waves of development sprang up in Pilsen in the early 2000s as I was growing up there.[5] Located just fifteen minutes from Chicago's central business district (known as the Loop) and directly adjacent to University Village, an upscale housing complex, and the University of Illinois at Chicago (UIC) campus, Pilsen was a target for city agencies and developers seeking new sites for redevelopment. With these initiatives came busses of real estate tourists and land speculators interested in cashing in on Pilsen's low cost of land and prime location near downtown, public transit, major highways, and local universities.[6] I saw new billboards with images of joyful, young, middle-class, seemingly White individuals and couples advertising "elite living" at prices that were forty times the going housing rates. At various intersections, construction signs were prominently displayed, with the tagline "Building a New Chicago" across an image of the city's flag (see Figure I.1).

Developers market possibility for those who can afford it, but signs of redevelopment promising a "better and new Chicago" and "elite living" raised questions for marginalized communities. This language indicated impending displacement and broken promises. As the artwork by Brian Herrera indicates, redevelopment often results in a newly gentrified city (Figure I.2). In Chicago, those most affected by such changes were residents of predominantly Black or Latina/o/x areas, neighborhoods that had experienced decades of government neglect—closed schools, concrete parks, unpaved roads, inadequate garbage disposal—together with violence, corruption, hyperpolicing, and unchecked crime. Many residents of these neighborhoods had themselves worked to transform their communities, engaging in grassroots mobilizations, partnering with the nonprofit sector, or using their own sweat, time, and money to clean up abandoned sites.

Yet in the city's portrayal of these neighborhoods as being in need of "redevelopment," Black and Latina/o/x residents' labor was often ignored, unrecognized, or even co-opted in the city's bid to attract

Figure I.I. "Building a New Chicago" sign underneath a railway. Photo by Teresa Irene Gonzales, July 5, 2018.

wealthier, often White residents to these areas. Simultaneously, it equated the residents of impoverished areas with urban neglect. This approach assumes that decayed neighborhoods are the result of impoverished, particularly Black and Brown residents' lack of upkeep or personal investment. This form of redevelopment led many residents and community organizers in my study to frustratingly exclaim, "This is why we can't have nice things!" The overwhelming sentiment was that any neighborhood improvements would ultimately benefit only incoming White, middle-class residents.

In this way, local efforts were rendered invisible, and the idea that these areas could be "improved" only through an influx of White residents was perpetuated. Throughout this book I showcase how Black and Mexican American residents from low-income communities, rather than devolving into apathetic mistrust or hopelessness, engage in acts of strategic mistrust, what I call collective skepticism, in order to lay claim to both their neighborhoods and the city.

Figure I.2. Artwork by artist Brian Herrera included in the *Peeling Off the Grey* exhibition at the National Museum of Mexican Art, which focused on analyzing the effects of gentrification on the Pilsen neighborhood. Curated by Teresa Magaña, May 11, 2018, to February 3, 2019. Photo by Teresa Irene Gonzales, June 19, 2018.

Urban Redevelopment: Growth-Based and Asset-Based Models

Historically, urban redevelopment strategies have further marginalized and excluded communities of color and poor residents from economic gains.[7] We see this pattern most clearly in neighborhood demolition campaigns (otherwise known as "slum clearance" or "urban renewal") and aggressive displacement of lower-income residents (both poor and lower middle class). When residents are displaced through such initiatives, they may lose access to affordable housing, good schools, and social networks and may experience increased social and economic isolation. These challenges are compounded by feelings of frustration and loss among Black and Latina/o/x residents who have worked hard to build safe environments in the face of implicitly racist city and state processes. Understanding this deep history of displacement and marginalization, cities started to approach redevelopment using a community-engaged process, which includes building relationships of trust between residents and the public and private sectors. The goal of this process is to create pathways for resident-inspired redevelopment that the neighborhood welcomes. However, history, redevelopment implementation, and continued displacement provide little incentive for marginalized populations to trust such redevelopment initiatives or the state.

To understand these challenges, it's first important to understand what redevelopment is: in the United States, it is the process by which cities and residents attempt to (re)imagine physical structures and available (i.e., vacant, abandoned, free) land. Throughout my research, I've identified two main approaches to it: growth-based and asset-based.

The Growth-Based Model

The growth-based model focuses on increasing an area's wealth by improving the built environment and the local business climate.[8] This approach includes such tactics as tax subsidies to keep businesses or attract them to a certain locale as well as beautification efforts and greening activities to improve a city's aesthetics. The theory is that an aesthetically pleasing city will attract wealthier and more highly skilled residents who can pay higher property taxes. These residents will also encourage the creation of a friendly business climate, which can lead to more jobs, increase competition, attract more businesses, and yield greater overall wealth for the area.

Gentrification is central to the growth model. This process of neighborhood turnover entails higher-income residents moving into lower-income areas of a city or town, often for access to a trendy neighborhood and/or more affordable housing or commercial property. The growth-model assumes that the "decay" of a neighborhood is the result of residents' neglect; it ignores the strides and improvements that existing residents have made in their own neighborhoods. It also ignores the contributions of *government* neglect. Indeed, in contrast with common assumptions, gentrification is not the passive result of organic resident movement, changing neighborhood tastes, or access to more affordable housing. Rather, politicians and city officials *choose* to leave these neighborhoods to decay, refusing to invest capital and/or time in maintaining, upgrading, or developing them until developers target one of them as the new hot place to live.

Again, this pattern is not passive—it is primarily the result of targeted efforts by state actors (municipal government), via growth-focused policies, and land use developers. These actors focus on capital reinvestment in order to (re)develop areas to attract higher-income residents, which means that wealthier people displace poorer people and diversity is replaced by social and cultural homogeneity. Within the United States, the continued disinvestment from neighborhoods with high concentrations of Black and Brown residents coupled with ongoing wealth inequality along racial lines often results in these same neighborhoods experiencing gentrification by mostly (though not always) wealthier Whites.[9]

As a result, gentrification both increases the inequality of power relations and exacerbates social isolation.[10] In a model where gentrification is conceived of as growth, redevelopment is assumed to be "good" for all parties involved, through increasing land values and the presence of a cleaner and safer environment. However, when a neighborhood gentrifies, housing costs increase (through rising rents and property taxes); in part as a result of a stagnant labor market and suppressed wages, the existing lower-income residents are displaced. Such displacement impacts more than housing choice; it also leads to the loss of social and cultural capital for existing low-income residents.[11] Additionally, such places lose what makes them unique and begin to look the same as each other—with the same shops, buildings, food, and so on—and working-class elements are demonized and/or removed in favor of specific aesthetic designs and certain economies.[12]

The Asset-Based Model

The second approach to redevelopment operates from an asset-based framework, which includes the various forms of local economic development.[13] These approaches are people- and place-based processes that focus on identifying local strengths and resources in order to transform or change local conditions to improve the quality of life for all residents (regardless of income). Rather than focusing on increases to outputs or transformation of physical landscapes and structures, asset-based development assesses the community as a whole. It emphasizes the development of land and physical structures, the local economies, and the people who reside in the area.[14]

This framework views residents as the owners of the area's development potential and as the benefactors of any development that occurs. As such, this approach relies heavily on resident input and engagement during the redevelopment process. Residents are asked to envision, dream, and design their ideal communities. The projects they propose might include attracting employers who will hire a high percentage of locals; developing affordable housing units; increasing resident ownership over public space, land, and small businesses; improving services and amenities; increasing jobs and other business opportunities; developing public goods such as parks; and increasing tax revenue.[15] Within Chicago, successful examples resulting from this approach include creating a local park on a brownfield site and working with residents to purchase empty and abandoned lots in their neighborhoods at a discount.[16] The idea is to increase local residents' access to wealth and ownership over local land and to decrease the potential for gentrification and displacement.

Another aspect of asset-based development focuses on increasing neighborhood social capital to support local endeavors. An example would be a small restaurant that employs local residents, trains youth from the local school in culinary arts, acquires its produce from a neighborhood-based farmer's market, banks at a local community bank, and has its menus printed by a local printer. Under asset-based development, increasing social capital and networking for resources is seen as a form of local self-sufficiency.

Although such asset-based redevelopment may seem comprehensive and community-focused, critics of this approach argue that residents are generally not trained in planning processes and can be easily swayed by charismatic politicians and technocrats to vote against their best interests.[17] Others acknowledge the benefits but claim that the approach is difficult to implement due to political and economic constraints, particularly in poor areas.[18]

Approaches to redevelopment rarely follow only one of these two models (or other emerging models)—generally, groups engage in a mix of asset-based and growth-based decisions. However, regardless of the approach to development, urban scholars such as Susan S. Fainstein argue that a strong civil society and a powerful grassroots sector are necessary to ensure equitable redevelopment.[19] Within urban communities, these elements will be strongest where there is an active presence of community-based organizations. The only times that redevelopment policies have proven more equitable across resident populations have been when they are developed in response to grassroots mobilization.[20] This is particularly true in Chicago, as we will explore in the coming sections.

Redevelopment and Community Organizing

For urban redevelopment, equitable solutions that include residents generally involve conversations with local grassroots and/or community-based nonprofits. Grassroots organizations are voluntary or nonprofit organizations that are composed of and by local residents; their members have weak or no ties to external funders. In contrast, community-based organizations are formal nonprofit organizations tied to specific geographic regions, such as neighborhoods.[21] They tend to focus on improving local conditions and the quality of life for residents and providing avenues for residents to escape poverty via social services and affordable housing units.[22] Local staff generally believe that residents have the most knowledge about what needs to be done in their own neighborhoods and therefore rely on community input in crafting neighborhood strategies.[23] Since the 1970s, such organizations have been at the center of development within poor inner-city communities.

The fact that they solicit community input, however, does not necessarily mean that community-based organizations are locally controlled; board members, directors, and professional staff do not always reside in the communities they serve, and their socioeconomic class or ethnoracial identity may be different from that of their constituents. Additionally, the development projects that community-based organizations encourage require money, staff, and technical expertise that are often not found within the community. As a result, they rely on external agencies (government, philanthropic foundations, private sector, and intermediaries) to help them reach their goals. These externally provided resources can create conflicts of interest for community organizations that wish to maintain grassroots ties.[24] For instance, funds awarded by many grant-making institutions (including philanthropic and governmental agencies) have strings attached that may not be in line with the receiving organization's mission, thereby requiring the group to choose between securing funding for their work and staying true to their mission.

Community-based nonprofits' reliance on such funds has also led some critics to argue that these organizations are disconnected from the communities they serve and that they operate as an extension of growth elites.[25] Foundations, for example, have been accused of supporting experimental programs that are politically sexy rather than essential mainstreamed services that community-based organizations already provide.[26] Critics argue that in such relationships strategies for neighborhood-based development become less about community involvement in decision making and more about achieving the funders' goals.[27]

"Welcome to Elite Living": Chicago Reenvisioned

Like most major urban areas, Chicago has a long history of neighborhood redevelopment. Development plans initially proceeded from local and state legislation, which in Illinois included the Neighborhood Redevelopment Corporation Act of 1941 (amended in 1953), the Blighted Areas Redevelopment Act of 1947, the Relocation Act of 1947, and the Urban Community Conservation Act of 1953. In the 1970s, the Chicago 21 Plan was implemented to revitalize areas surrounding the central business district. This plan affected parts of the Near West Side around the current UIC campus and areas north of the downtown central business district.[28] Previous redevelopment initiatives in Chicago followed a top-down technocratic approach, with the mayor's office in control of all decision making. At the dawn of the new millennium, however, changes in philanthropy coupled with a changing political landscape encouraged new forms of redevelopment to emerge.[29] Central to these initiatives was an attempt to integrate input from the business world, community nonprofits, academics, the local government, and area residents.

One such initiative was the New Communities Program, a ten-year, multimillion-dollar project that brought together city officials, the John D. and Catherine T. MacArthur Foundation, a national community development intermediary (specifically the Chicago office of the Local Initiatives Support Corporation), and local community-based organizations.[30] The Local Initiatives Support Corporation used plans developed with the Banana Kelly Community Improvement Association in the Fort Apache neighborhood of the South Bronx in New York City as a model for the New Communities Program.[31] In an effort to ensure the availability of quality, affordable housing in the Bronx, Banana Kelly partnered with other area community organizations and the Local Initiatives Support Corporation to develop a coalitional model of community-based development. This ensured a comprehensive and scaled approach to redevelopment that could have a lasting impact. Drawing on lessons learned from Banana Kelly and other initiatives in high-poverty, Latina/o/x and African American areas of New York City, the New Communities Program underscored the importance of research, social capital (through building trust relationships), self-help, public-private partnerships, and local accountability.

In operation between 2002 and 2013, the New Communities Program was part of the strategy to achieve a larger, Chicago-wide goal: to reenvision development across communities of color that experienced enduring poverty and crime. The $900 million initiative involved sixteen neighborhoods, all predominantly African American and/or Latina/o/x. It aimed to (1) increase the capacities of neighborhood nonprofits, (2) address the historical exclusion of poor Black and Latina/o/x residents from large-scale redevelopment initiatives, (3) build deep relationships of trust between low-income communities of color and city hall, and (4) use Chicago as a test case for the Local Initiatives Support Corporation to develop a model of "comprehensive community development," which was later used nationally across partner cities. Initial conversations regarding this large-scale redevelopment occurred during the 1996 Futures Forum. This yearlong series of meetings and discussions focused on community development work in Chicago was spearheaded by the MacArthur Foundation and by an organization that had solidified itself as the go-to expert on local economic development in the United States: the Local Initiatives Support Corporation.

Founded in 1979 through a major grant from the Ford Foundation, the Local Initiatives Support Corporation operates as a national intermediary between the corporate community, banks, local government, and nonprofits representing local neighborhoods.[32] As of 2019, the organization operates in thirty-five major cities, twenty-two states,

Washington, D.C., and hundreds of rural areas across the United States.[33] The corporation assembles private and public funds and directs them toward local communities via community-based nonprofits, which then design and implement targeted development strategies. It is not, however, a community-organizing organization; its sole mission is to increase and implement local economic development in low-income areas.[34]

This organization collaborated with city officials, the John D. and Catherine T. MacArthur Foundation, and local community-based organizations to create the New Communities Program. Drawing on twenty years of community development experience and the expertise of development professionals, this program combined elements that included a comprehensive process for quality-of-life planning, training on relationship building, and socialization of neighborhood nonprofits into a specific model and professional mode of doing business. It attempted to address both human and physical development projects. Goals encompassed developing local resources, improving conditions and quality of life for residents, and supporting local change agents as neighborhood innovators.

Since the implementation of Chicago's New Communities Program, the model has expanded, as the Building Sustainable Communities Program, to sixty-three areas across the United States, with physical redevelopment, community safety efforts, and workforce development in high-poverty areas in Indianapolis, Olneyville (in Providence, Rhode Island), and North Philadelphia.[35] In addition to speaking to the success of the model, this expansion further solidifies the Local Initiatives Support Corporation as the national expert on comprehensive local economic development.

A History of Government Involvement with Urban Redevelopment

The New Communities Program is emblematic of the antipoverty and urban renewal campaigns of the twentieth century; in its focus on public-private partnerships, it has extended their legacy.[36] During the 1960s, the Johnson administration launched an array of federal programs that focused on comprehensive community development. These programs provided support for local activism and institution building and formed a new network of nonprofit providers and intermediary organizations that were committed to community development.[37] The programs included Community Action, Model Cities, and the Special Impact Program. The Community Action Program's chief objective was local social service reform. Although it provided a number of services, the program did not provide a pathway to jobs, which was badly needed in the low-income areas it served. This was largely due to the Johnson administration's view that targeted job creation was unnecessary and too expensive. In order to provide a solution to issues of continued poverty, federal policy makers came up with two additional programs: Model Cities and Special Impact. These two programs were aimed at areas with concentrations of poor minorities. The Ford Foundation invested in the Model Cities program, which combined services with brick-and-mortar programs, all the while giving planning control to city officials.[38]

Although flawed, Model Cities was able to concentrate funds in the poorest neighborhoods because of its targeting plan.[39] Whereas Model Cities used a combination of service delivery and programming, the Special Impact Program was meant to revitalize poor communities through economic development, but with a services and training component as well. It provided block grants to community nonprofits; they in turn would design, finance, and administer their own development strategies. According to historian Alice O'Connor, these programs were too limited in scope and funding to alter inequities or combat the high levels of stratification that segregated poor places.[40] That being said, the basic framework of these programs continues to shape the strategies that neighborhood nonprofits, philanthropic groups, and policy makers implement in low-income areas.

The New Communities Program built upon these previous initiatives by incorporating a multifaceted and comprehensive approach that combined social service programming and physical redevelopment. The program connected multiple issues across policy arenas (for instance, housing, commerce, land use, and education). It built relationships across government, philanthropy, and Chicago's local nonprofits and made the neighborhood the focus for addressing poverty.

With the implementation of the New Communities Program, Chicago attempted to take a collaborative approach to development within low-income communities. This focus included resident input at specific stages of the program. Still, past redevelopment efforts have generally favored developers and business interests, so residents of low-income neighborhoods, regardless of community-engagement efforts, have little faith that any redevelopment gains will benefit them or their communities.[41] This is particularly true for residents on Chicago's South and West sides, where aldermanic support is low, poverty and crime rates are high, and abandoned buildings, boarded-up houses, and empty storefronts are pervasive.

Urban Redevelopment and Systemic Inequality

I came to this project as a result of my frustration with the scholarly literature, which too often ignores Latina/o/x populations and often depicts the poor and people of color as victims, criminals, and passive recipients of urban policies. From my own experiences, I knew that poor, urban Black and Mexican American communities are organized, complex spaces. Additionally, I had witnessed other, more positive kinds of engagement, such as people collectively addressing social issues (through neighborhood cleanup drives, food distribution, and local actions to increase equality), exhibiting an entrepreneurial spirit (selling trinkets in the laundromats or *tamales, champurrado*, and sliced fruit on the streets), and just going about their days. I don't share these examples to valorize or romanticize poor communities of color; I show instead, and as urbanists like Drake and Cayton, Du Bois, Isoke, Patillo, Rios, and Sánchez-Jankowski have revealed, that impoverished communities of color navigate and influence cities in complex ways.

To do so, it's essential to contend with institutional violence in this context, and several timely and important texts do exactly that. Sociologist Robert Vargas's *Wounded City: Violent Turf Wars in a Chicago Barrio* is an excellent recent example.[42] It highlights the various ways that spatial redistricting of ward boundaries, which Vargas terms "political turf wars," impacts neighborhood gang violence. As he explains, decisions made by city hall deeply impact the interactions between neighborhood organizations, from nonprofits to churches, public schools, and local gangs. Rethinking the impact of competition over limited resources (including space and land) on neighborhood dynamics is key to understanding a variety of urban issues, from poverty to violence and redevelopment.

Such rethinking can help explain the challenges and opportunities in Chicago neighborhoods, which contain not only criminal and violent elements but also those working to mobilize communities, disrupt histories of dispossession, and provide alternative pathways to low-income residents of color. And resident mobilization around urban redevelopment is not unique to Chicago—it is evident in the work done in places like Detroit, Houston, Boston, and New York. For example, in Houston resident mobilization within the historic African American Third Ward has led to a large-scale urban arts community that includes affordable housing, youth mentorship, and increased community ownership.[43] Similarly, in New York City Puerto Rican community organizations have been integral to fighting for equitable redevelopment initiatives in relation to affordable housing and environmental justice.[44] Akin to groups in these other contexts, Black and Latina/o/x residents in Chicago strategically mobilize to ensure equitable redevelopment initiatives and to problematize stereotypical conceptions of low-income people within marginalized communities.

Chicago as the Vanguard of New Development

I first saw this project through the lens of gentrification, but my focus soon expanded to encompass the impact of larger redevelopment processes on marginalized populations. I came to realize that, more than any other urban processes, redevelopment and city planning consistently frame, drive, and inform many other forms of systemic inequality, particularly as they relate to race and class. They do so via zoning laws, the location of polluting industries vis-à-vis poor communities of color, the closure of public schools, the location of new businesses, and so on. All of these decisions emerge from meticulous, large-scale planning decisions at the city level, but the people so often making them do not represent the vast majority of urban residents affected.

Although I was interested in these ideas more broadly, I wanted to study Chicago in particular. This is a city that is predominantly both Mexican and Black with a strong history of grassroots mobilization and a healthy philanthropic and nonprofit presence. African Americans and Latinas/os/xs constitute nearly two-thirds of Chicago's population, often live close to each other, and contend with the same issues of political and economic disenfranchisement, racialized narratives regarding poverty and violence, environmental racism, and restricted access to full citizenship within the city. However, little comparative research analyzes how Blacks and Latinas/os/xs mobilize around their economic and political disenfranchisement, particularly as it relates to redevelopment. Given the New Communities Program's focus on building relationships of trust, I was particularly curious about what this means within marginalized communities marked by long histories of disinvestment.

One of the most important drivers of this research appeared when I first learned about the New Communities Program in the summer of 2008, while interviewing small business owners in Pilsen. I was attempting to understand the impact of gentrification on the strong local ethnic economy. During many of the interviews, participants referenced the New Communities Program and highlighted big changes anticipated in the neighborhood. One informant in particular, a director of a local community development corporation, asserted that, to weather the impending development, the Mexican community would "have to grab the gentrification bull by its horns." This executive director understood that urban redevelopment to attract wealthier residents was inevitable.

Still, he refused to passively watch this process lead to the displacement of a historically rich Mexican American enclave. Instead, he and other nonprofit staff in the community began to coordinate efforts in an attempt to ensure that the Mexican history and culture of the neighborhood remained. If, as sociologist Frederick F. Wherry contends, "people and the places they inhabit carry memories and meanings and invite emotional attachment," what does that mean for populations who know that redevelopment, and potentially displacement, is inevitable?[45] This study is an attempt to understand how locally based groups—and the partners they choose—contend with impending urban redevelopment. I pay particular attention to relationships of trust because they are rooted within systems of power and inequality, but ultimately this is a story of Black and Mexican American nonprofit staff and grassroots activists and their strategic attempts to redirect resources and increase gains to their communities in ways that *they* consider to be important. Although both groups navigate systems of institutional racism and classism, this book focuses primarily on collective responses to urban redevelopment initiatives. This is not to say that race and class are not important; rather, in focusing on collective responses I demonstrate how marginalized populations strategically navigate power relations.[46]

Interorganizational Trust and Redevelopment

Building a Better Chicago explores the complex ecosystem of nonprofits within the city and highlights the tensions between formal nonprofits and informal grassroots organizations. As scholars of urban neighborhoods argue, such field-level analysis allows us to more fully understand how relationships between community members within the neighborhood (i.e., those who are endogenous to the system) and external agencies and groups (i.e., those who are exogenous to the system) frame neighborhood dynamics.[47] Throughout the text, I analyze how urban elites, nonprofit staff, and residents use interorganizational trust and mistrust to respond to large-scale redevelopment initiatives. As part of this, I developed the term "collective skepticism" to better understand the ways that community organizations within marginalized communities engage in strategic collective mistrust. The book centers on the aforementioned ten-year redevelopment project—the New Communities Program—in two key high-poverty Black and Mexican American neighborhoods of Chicago, Greater Englewood and Little Village.

This work bridges an important gap in the urban redevelopment literature by showcasing how distinct community organizations negotiate disparate power relationships through local campaigns. Much of the literature focuses on organizations in isolation or on individual group responses to urban development.[48] In this book I highlight the ways that groups strategically rely on urban networks to navigate power structures. I pay particular attention to the differences and similarities between Black-led and Mexican-led grassroots organizations that strategically use collective skepticism to influence redevelopment initiatives within their neighborhoods. I offer insight into how redevelopment policy is implemented on the ground, articulate the political and social benefits of collective skepticism, and critique the partial perspectives dominant in social capital and community development studies.

The findings challenge prevailing urban theories, which highlight the denigrative impacts of mistrust within poor neighborhoods while promoting the importance of trust between neighborhood-based nonprofits and municipal governments. In contrast with those theories, I argue that organizational trust is not always a positive force—rather, it can be co-opted as a mode of control, used to minimize dissent and to socialize members into a homogenous organizational culture. Furthermore, I demonstrate how organizational mistrust, or collective skepticism, can yield a number of positive outcomes. Such skepticism can be used to engage residents and local and national nonprofits to pressure city officials into improving neighborhood quality of life. In this way, it serves as a tool for safeguarding resident-led planning processes, expanding collaborative organizational networks, building leadership among local residents, and transforming negative perceptions of the neighborhoods in question.

I show that a combination of trust and mistrust is a rational and productive response to urban policies and state actors who attempt to direct the benefits of redevelopment toward urban elites and away from the communities themselves.

1

Àse

(Mis)trust, Change Makers, and Leadership Development in Two Chicago Neighborhoods

What we fundamentally want to do is tackle this racist, problematic, culturally divisive, and classist land use plan that is displacing our communities.
—Destina Kunze, 2016

In the early 2000s, Ernie Jones was a consistent leader of community meetings across the city of Chicago. A longtime community activist and executive director of a university-based community engagement center, he pursued twin passions: the arts within communities of color and racial unity between the Black and Brown populations of Chicago. The community meetings that he convened several times a month reflected both of these passions and attracted activists interested in music, poetry, history, public space, and economic development. Before each meeting, attendees would check in by sitting in a circle and briefly introducing themselves, and Ernie would make sure that they collectively greeted each other with the word *àse*.

A Yoruba philosophical concept, *àse* (sometimes spelled *ashe*) partly connotes the power and willingness of community members to create change. For Ernie, this word served as a powerful reminder of the purpose of each meeting as well as a call to focus when a meeting drifted off topic. Ernie used *àse* as a framework for his activism and as a principle for mentoring others interested in deep societal change. For him, this concept was central to ensuring social and economic justice for marginalized residents of Chicago. During our many conversations, Ernie and I discussed this approach to community-engaged work.

Sitting in his cramped office filled with African and African American artwork in an affluent North Side neighborhood, Ernie raised issues of trust, engagement, and resident skepticism around city-led redevelopment. Considering his thirty-plus-year career of community organizing on the South and Southwest sides of Chicago, he reflected on the long history of foundations and city officials who had ignored the capacities of Black- and Brown-led neighborhood groups. For Ernie, disregarding the contributions of residents highlighted a very real divide between neighborhood groups and downtown elites. Government officials, Ernie highlighted, have little interest in engaging and empowering poor Black and Latina/o/x residents, who might disrupt their visions for the city. I asked specifically about the New Communities Program, the citywide redevelopment project. Ernie sighed deeply and said, "It's a shadow—if you will—of what's to come. At the beck and call of the mayor . . . people don't trust them, and that's okay."

Over nearly three years of research that spanned from 2011 to 2016 on community organizations in Chicago, I came to understand this remark. Frequently, I heard rampant mistrust of community nonprofits and local government blamed for a number of negative unintended consequences. Mistrust, I was told by residents, city officials, development experts, and community activists, was a cause of retrenched poverty, increased gang activity, inadequate coalition building, and lower quality education systems. When discussing the challenges that community organizations faced with regard to collaboration, I heard comments like "Issues of trust? It's all about competition for funding, competition for community leadership. It's about perceptions of power and leadership" and "Everyone has their own agendas. They're shady. They're not committed to the neighborhood. It exacerbates [mis]trust." As I continued my fieldwork, both tensions and discourse regarding trust and mistrust regularly bubbled to the surface. Most people lamented the lack of trust in their communities. Similarly, city officials and staff from the Local Initiatives Support Corporation (the national community development intermediary involved in the program) regularly commented on a lack of trust in poor Black and Latina/o/x communities. Several of the people I came to know over the five years I worked in Chicago highlighted money, ego, and political affiliation as significant in perpetuating mistrust among organizations.

Yet because I had spent time in each community, working alongside activists and nonprofit staff, attending meetings, and observing behaviors, I noticed a clear disconnect between discourse and actions. Yes, people stated regularly that trust was lacking in Little Village and Greater Englewood, but I saw people working together strategically, even when they did not trust other organizations or the city. Reflecting on Ernie's "that's okay" comment led me to reconsider mistrust in community development. How, I wondered, can all of this mistrust coexist with a community sentiment like *àse*? How does mistrust operate with a community's efforts for change? As I asked these questions, my theory of collective skepticism began taking root.

Valorizing Trust

Community leaders like Ernie understand that achieving their wider goals requires partnerships with powerful funders, foundations, developers, city hall officials, and economic elites. Meanwhile, city leaders—particularly those involved in redevelopment projects in low-income communities—must inspire at least a modicum of community participation for their work to be considered legitimate. Both groups, then, need each other. Their relationship, however, is hardly egalitarian. In this context, trust is commonly understood to be the basis for a productive relationship, a precondition for effective interaction between social actors engaged in community development.

Indeed, scholars who study communities tend to highlight the many benefits of trust and the many negative consequences of mistrust.[1] Such scholars as well as many public figures blame a lack of trust for creating barriers to community building and for contributing to negative outcomes in impoverished areas. How can any community project, they argue, succeed without establishing trust among all involved? African American and Latina/o/x urban residents, however, may have a different view. Their perspectives are often very much informed by a long history of redevelopment projects in poorer areas, and based on their experiences, their trust is not so easy to come by.

How can we understand trust? The literature on trust highlights a social actor's expectation of vulnerability, together with certain rules of behavior. Trust is a profoundly social act: it allows actors to build cooperative relationships and to take risks that may be mutually beneficial. In the process, those who trust assume a degree of "uncertainty regarding motives and prospective actions" or the "ability to monitor or control that other party."[2] This vulnerability is particularly salient in relationships involving unequal partners and the exchange of valuable resources, such as technical expertise, money, or political clout.[3] A person who trusts may expect that trust not to be abused but also understands the potential for harm. Trust is thus simultaneously a hope, a risk, and a way of acting toward others.

Trust is important for expanding networks of social support, gaining access to much-needed resources, and engaging in the flow of information. At the neighborhood level, scholars find, communities with high levels of trust generally have higher levels of employment, lower high school dropout rates, greater appeal to people both inside and outside the neighborhood, and higher rates of civic engagement.[4] For nonprofits, grassroots organizations, and resident associations, trust among organizations helps to build capacity, leverage existing resources, and acquire new ones, including access to skills, credibility, information, and money through loans, grants, and other financial assistance.[5] These resources, in turn, subsidize operating costs and the salaries of nonprofit employees. Studies of organizational trust in corporate, nonprofit, and community settings thus focus on the benefits of increasing organizational trust and building interorganizational networks.[6]

Trust and Social Capital

Much research shows that trust between organizations increases access to resources and helps underresourced groups get things done.[7] But trust alone is insufficient—to accomplish their goals, communities also need high levels of social capital.

Social capital is defined as the relationships through which groups, organizations, and individuals access resources (e.g., money, expertise, access to housing, information about a job, a delicious recipe). People access and build social capital through work, school, houses of worship, family, and neighborhood connections, as well as through a range of particular activities. It increases as networks of people and organizations expand to encompass new and different connections or information. Such diverse connections are key—if everyone in a community has the same information, each individual's social capital remains low, even if community members all trust each other. High levels of social capital require new information filtering in from a variety of sources.

We can understand social capital as encompassing four main components: socialization into established beliefs, reciprocity, bounded solidarity, and enforceable trust.[8] In much of the literature, however, scholars often point to trust as a central ingredient for increasing the social capital necessary for social cohesion and collaboration. For example, sociologists Mario Small and Sandra Smith highlight trust as a hallmark of social capital and deem it essential for facilitating access to assets and resources.[9] Analysts of community development likewise assume trust to be central to increasing social capital.[10] This perceived link leads academics and policy makers to promote trust in marginalized communities that can benefit from the flow of social capital. By increasing information and resources to these communities, they assert, poor inner-city or racially marginalized residents and local organizations can overcome neighborhood poverty.

Although social capital seems like an inherently good thing, as sociologists Alejandro Portes, Julia Sensenbrenner, and Robert Putnam highlight, it can also have an insidious underbelly: social capital can be used to consolidate economic or political power in the hands of the few.[11] The same can be said of trust, particularly between groups with unequal access to social, economic, and political power.[12] In focusing on only the benefits of trust, therefore, we ignore its dark side: within networks encompassing power inequities, trust can replicate and solidify social and racial injustices. Whereas trust between equals can open up access to new opportunities, it can pose special risks for those on the margins.

From Trust to Mistrust

In interviews and in casual conversations with me, local activists often recalled a history that most policy makers know well. They would tell me of 1950s urban renewal programs that destroyed neighborhoods, displaced communities, and disrupted social networks with little regard for those who lived there, most of whom were poor African American, Mexican, and Puerto Rican residents. They would tell me about programs—Community Action, Model Cities, the Special Impact Program, and the Community Development Block Grant—that were all unsuccessful responses to segregation and inequality. Such initiatives may have provided support for local activism and institution building, I heard, and they may have formed a basis for equitable community development. But residents saw them as limited, ineffective half measures. Neighborhood activists thus saw recent redevelopment initiatives, such as empowerment zones and tax increment financing districts as merely the latest schemes promoted by elected officials and urban elites and feared that these initiatives, like earlier ones, would increase gentrification and contribute to their marginalization.

Considering the perspectives of poor communities of color, who questioned initiatives for planning and redevelopment, alongside those of the powerful, who promoted and expected trust, led me to wonder about this idea of "trust," considered both so crucial and so elusive. What if trust, rather than binding groups together, serves as a wedge to keep them apart? What if trust, rather than promoting empowerment, consolidates power with established elites and scuttles effective neighborhood development? How might trust, however laudable, also marginalize less powerful voices and blame victims of long-standing systems of inequality? Might there be, somewhat counterintuitively, benefits to *mis*trust among community organizations?

Mistrust and Collective Skepticism

Urban development scholars and public figures alike blame a lack of trust for creating barriers to community building and increasing negative outcomes in impoverished Black and Latina/o/x areas. Like poverty, mistrust is pathologized as individual weakness, indicative of a flawed character. It is treated as a collective disease that must be contained and remedied. To explain its persistence in low-income communities of color marked by decay and disinvestment, those who study mistrust racialize it: according to scholarship on urban development and poverty, mistrust develops among poor Black and Latina/o/x residents who feel powerless, lack access to resources, and reside in disadvantaged neighborhoods with high levels of crime, poverty, and social disorder.[13] Mistrust, therefore, is understood as an extension of powerlessness, exacerbated by social isolation, in areas where neighborhood institutions that might provide social and economic support are only minimally effective or else entirely absent. These studies often situate mistrust at the community level, where poor residents—usually of color—mistrust both their neighbors and their local institutions, such as government, the education system, and the criminal justice system.

Urban sociologist Sandra Smith challenges this notion that scarcity of resources breeds mistrust.[14] She highlights that poor Blacks do develop relationships of trust and cooperation. Likewise, in her research on policing, Monica Bell argues that Black mothers engage in situational trust with police officers when necessary.[15] Similarly, in his study of child care centers in New York City, Mario Small finds poor neighbors relying on each other for means, safety, housework, child care, transportation, and information.[16] In the face of scarce resources and needs, people develop informal arrangements that, out of necessity, generate networks of exchange. These networks require at least a minimum level of trust. Scarcity can thus lead to trust, and despite skepticism, individual needs in such situations can outweigh feelings of mistrust.

Although other studies provide important insight into the ways that mistrust can exacerbate the conditions of poverty, their focus on the negative impacts of mistrust can obfuscate the structural conditions— whether social, political, or economic—that lead to mistrust among residents of marginalized spaces.[17] Such a focus also pathologizes mistrust as a condition and extension of racialized poverty and further places the onus on residents to adjust their behaviors, both toward each other and toward the institutions they encounter. Rather than viewing mistrust simply as an outcome of oppression, however, we must instead see it as a logical reaction to local circumstances and constraints that are shaped by oppression.[18] As Eddie Glaude reminds us, "There is a deep-seated skepticism of the moral capacity of White people—rooted in histories of dispossession, racism, and anti-Black [and Latinx] policies and actions."[19] This skepticism or mistrust is a logical response by communities of color to implicit and explicit structural racism in which institutions and Whiteness become synonymous.

To further explore this idea, consider that instead of viewing mistrust as the opposite of trust, we might identify both conditions on a continuum, where one cannot exist without the other. First, consider that trust varies in both nature and degree depending on the relationship. When we trust someone, we expect an element of reciprocity—that is, we expect the trusted person to act in ways that align with our interests. However, we don't expect the same kind of reciprocity from our employers that we expect from our friends or family members. Likewise, our level of trust differs based on the relationship. Mistrust operates in that same way.

Note that organizations do not themselves trust in the same ways that individuals trust—rather, they consolidate power and seek relationships that can further their goals.[20] Organizations lack the vulnerability of individuals and cannot reciprocate an individual's action. In the context of urban redevelopment, organizations often align their plans, projects, and agendas with those of development elites and, ultimately, with municipal wishes. Whatever their individual levels of trust, residents are not the primary participants or goal setters in urban planning. As such, they have very little reason to trust that organizations—including community-based ones—have the same goals as community members.

Collective Skepticism as Rational Mistrust

The heavy focus on increasing relationships of trust within poor communities of color has led many scholars to ignore the ways that mistrust is both rational and useful. With few exceptions, studies overlook the power differentials that operate between local groups and within organizational networks.[21] From a stream of organizational studies associated with the "new institutionalism," we know that interorganizational networks operate within a system of power that, once institutionalized, can actually preserve power imbalances.[22] Yet by focusing principally on the perceived benefits and goodwill that trust can offer and by assuming that inner-city organizations and residents have the same goals as each other, we fail to build knowledge about the impact of power differentials within networks and develop little understanding of the ways that community-based agencies navigate power structures. This lack of understanding creates challenges because these power differentials heavily influence decisions and actions, often to the detriment of the community.

However, if we instead focus on organizational relationships, such as through a field-level analysis, we can gain a more nuanced understanding of how organizations operate and the processes they undertake that may further marginalize disempowered populations, particularly poor communities of color, that may justify mistrust.[23] Attention to organizational fields—which we can understand as sets of organizations within a given area of focus and that include interdependent relationships between public and private organizations—allows us to consider the diversity of organizations that interact and, potentially, influence each other. It also clarifies that organizations within a particular field are often constrained by institutional structures and that they may, in turn, act in ways that reproduce those structures. For example, if a nonprofit director knows that her organization will receive funding for focusing on the beautification of a small business district as opposed to funding for advocating for policy changes to commercial leases, she may redirect the mission of her nonprofit to the fundable beautification projects.

Organizations are not "free floating islands of rationality"—they are social and cultural systems embedded within an institutional context.[24] As such, they are seriously constrained by social expectations and properties of legitimacy.[25] Externally created norms, values, and institutions have a major impact on their behavior and structure. This institutional context may create a culture that defines social relations between members.[26]

Such organizational culture is driven by an understanding of control that affects not only interorganizational structures but also the strategy of each actor in an organizational field.[27] Within the area of redevelopment, organizational fields are shaped by historical context (including past relationships and previous redevelopment attempts), the interests involved (public and private entities and local residents), and new theories and practices regarding development. Although urban elites—including elected officials, development experts, and private entities—can dictate many redevelopment decisions, a community with a strong civic sector can influence those decisions to ensure that more equitable development occurs.

As evidenced in Chicago, rather than relying on trust or mistrust to mediate these relationships, community groups that represent racially marginalized populations within interorganizational networks can use what I term *collective skepticism* to more equitably shift power dynamics and influence development decisions.

Collective skepticism—or strategic collective mistrust, through which a community charges elites with proving they are trustworthy—is a tactical tool that draws on the expertise of community organizers, harnessing their knowledge of local development decisions and the processes that have shaped development in their neighborhoods. Rather than encouraging residents to trust a process that has historically excluded them, community workers who use this tool can require that urban development plans—whether created by the city, local foundations, or a combination of entities—detail efforts to include and support low-income residents. Central to collective skepticism is an understanding that (1) trust is situated within structures of power and (2) organizations and residents do not, necessarily, have the same goals. Explained this way, it is clear that collective skepticism is not the opposite of trust. It simply recognizes that relationships with urban elites can be both beneficial and detrimental to low-income communities of color, and it allows organizations to leverage that recognition to achieve goals for a given community.

For community groups in conflict with government and municipal policies, collective skepticism can be a valuable tool in the fight against ongoing neighborhood exploitation. This tool helps to create social and symbolic boundaries and diminish social cohesion between organizations with disparate access to power. Social cohesion is often viewed as a positive component for increasing trust, building community, decreasing marginalization, and expanding opportunities. It absolutely provides benefits to group members with similar goals. However, social cohesion can also operate to reify power imbalances—through consensus building—particularly in redevelopment initiatives. Conversely, using collective skepticism to buffer social cohesion, activists and residents are less likely to comply with group expectations that may not actually benefit most residents. In this way, collective skepticism affirms often-ignored histories of exclusionary urban policies and their effects on marginalized populations, linking histories of dispossession with elite modes of partnership. These processes are particularly useful when scarce resources, power inequities, and dwindling external funding compel community groups to work with external agencies.

Through collective skepticism, community organizers can effectively use mistrust to promote resident empowerment and ensure that local partners uphold equity in development projects.

Collective Skepticism: An Organizing Tool

I began to think about mistrust as I witnessed members of various organizations strategically using both trust and mistrust as tools for addressing issues in neighborhood development. Regarding a range of issues—from attracting economic resources to expanding the capacities of local nonprofits, from providing youth programming to holding politicians accountable—I saw folks assume a position of collective skepticism. Like the "organized skepticism" that sociologist Robert K. Merton describes within scientific communities, some community organizers within Black and Latina/o/x communities similarly approach their work from a place of mistrust.[28] Whereas Merton was discussing science's ability to threaten and disrupt existing power structures because of a desire to uncover truths, community organizers in my study had the courage to challenge existing beliefs and ideologies within a dominant society that neither supports their work nor values frameworks emerging from their impoverished Black and Latina/o/x communities. Their position comes from a place of historically racialized marginalization and oppression, so like Merton's scientists, they use skepticism to expose different truths that are often ignored and silenced. This framework allowed them to fight power with power.[29]

Applying collective skepticism with their own contexts, these actors strategically used trust and mistrust to create what I term *networks of opportunity* between organizations with disparate economic and political power. These networks provided collaborative relationships for local community groups engaged with urban power elites. By maintaining collective skepticism, locals could navigate tricky relationships with elites for their own organizations and constituents and, in the process, mitigate the threat of co-optation.

Networks of opportunity are, in essence, weak ties, which are exactly the kinds of ties needed in the context of neighborhood redevelopment. Although the term may seem to signify connections that lack in power or strength, weak ties actually provide individuals with a variety of resources. They diffuse ideas, serve as bridges between individuals and different groups, and provide access to new information and other resources outside one's social circle.[30] Extending this idea of weak ties, networks of opportunity arise as a situational and collective response to achieving equitable neighborhood redevelopment. Such ties allow for pragmatic collaboration between organizations that lack relationships of trust but that have similar goals or need access to specific opportunities. In developing temporary networks of these types to address common goals, organizers can avoid calls for blindly engaging in trust relations and still work together to achieve their goals. This approach to collaboration can promote heterogeneous plans, minimize socialization into a homogenous organizational culture, and reduce power differentials between residents, community groups, and redevelopment elites who control decision making.

Community groups that engage in collective skepticism share some unique behaviors: They demand inclusion in all processes of development, from planning to implementation and studying of impacts. They further expect their partners to submit to critical inquiry regarding new and ongoing projects. Eager to learn about development processes and to share their knowledge, these community groups educate themselves and become more adept at identifying worthwhile projects.

In Chicago, I saw collective skepticism being used to address diverse goals: to build leadership among local residents, to safeguard resident-led planning processes, to expand coalitional organizational networks, to transform locally negative perceptions of neighborhoods, to pressure city officials to improve neighborhood quality of life, to engage residents with local and national nonprofits, and to advocate for increased access to public transit, green spaces, and pollution controls. Collective skepticism offers a key to accessing the opportunities and avoiding the pitfalls of working across social and symbolic boundaries and across gulfs of political and economic power.

Case Study: Community Groups and Redevelopment

This book analyzes the ways that community groups in predominantly Black and Mexican American neighborhoods of Chicago used trust and collective skepticism as strategic tools in pursuing their goals for neighborhood development. Drawing on thirty months of participant observation in six community organizations in two Chicago neighborhoods, I reveal the processes through which engaging in relationships of trust between organizational actors with unequal power can socialize some community-based organizations into a framework that delegitimized conflict-oriented grassroots organizing. The result was a series of local solutions that did provide resources to impoverished residents but that nonetheless failed to challenge governmental decisions that perpetuated racialized systems of poverty. As other Chicago-based organizers demonstrated, however, such dynamics are not inevitable—it is also possible for community organizations to use both trust and mistrust, via collective skepticism, to mitigate such power differentials between organizational actors and to train residents to challenge unjust government policies. Tensions between organizations that engaged in relationships of trust and those that deployed collective skepticism to develop networks of opportunity were particularly noticeable in the New Communities Program, which, as described in the introduction, was a large-scale redevelopment initiative that took place between 2002 and 2013.

The New Communities Program

The New Communities Program was part of the work to achieve a larger goal: to reenvision development within Chicago. To that end, the national community development intermediary involved in the program—the Local Initiatives Support Corporation—aimed to transform sixteen distressed or vulnerable neighborhoods into areas that have jobs that provide a living wage, have successful business corridors, and are safe environments, with low levels of crime.[31] Tables 1.1 and 1.2 provide an overview of the demographics of the sixteen neighborhoods in 2000, just before the New Communities Program started, and in 2009, toward the end of the initiative.[32] As can be seen in the tables, neighborhoods with high percentages of African American and/or Latina/o/x populations saw comparable high rates of poverty and low rates of educational attainment across the decade. With few exceptions—and hardly surprising given the impact of the 2007–8 recession and the foreclosure crisis on communities of color in Chicago—residents of these areas were worse off in 2009. As indicated in its mission, the New Communities Program had the potential to transform blighted and ignored communities for existing residents. This work, however, centered on community buy-in and support from city hall.

TABLE 1.1. 2000 census tract data for the sixteen New Communities Program neighborhoods

Neigh-borhood	Commu-nity area	Latina/o/x or Hispanic %	White %	Black %	Housing vacancy %	Below federal poverty line %	18–24 no high school diploma %
Logan Square	22	65.08	26.29	5.19	8.25	19.80	34.82
Humboldt Park	23	48.01	3.32	47.40	10.10	31.11	45.58
East Gar-field Park	27	0.99	1.13	97.20	14.60	35.18	39.57
West Haven	28	2.17	2.14	94.06	14.58	48.42	37.78
North Lawndale	29	4.54	0.92	93.77	15.17	45.18	39.08
Little Village	30	83.03	3.52	12.91	8.47	26.52	55.39
Pilsen	31	88.90	8.15	1.76	11.19	26.96	46.95
Douglas	35	1.11	6.59	85.51	20.53	41.25	14.48
Oakland	36	0.95	0.65	97.50	20.67	52.46	24.40
Grand Boulevard	38	0.84	0.62	97.73	27.36	46.90	44.50
North Kenwood	39	0.94	1.22	96.58	21.97	38.52	30.49
Washing-ton Park	40	0.95	0.52	97.54	22.93	51.64	41.63
Woodlawn	42	1.06	2.81	94.21	14.89	39.42	31.92
South Chicago	46	27.37	2.94	68.02	12.35	29.71	37.36
Chicago Lawn	66	35.06	10.08	52.50	7.68	19.76	36.39
West Engle-wood[a]	67	1.01	0.36	97.77	12.04	32.13	37.64
Engle-wood	68	0.86	0.44	97.84	17.03	43.80	41.82
Auburn-Gresham	71	0.62	0.42	98.09	8.44	20.61	32.55

[a] Not included in the New Communities Program; I include it here because residents of Greater Englewood view it as one neighborhood (Englewood and West Englewood).
Data compiled using census tract information from the 2000 United States Census.

TABLE 1.2. 2009 American Community Survey census tract data for the sixteen New Communities Program neighborhoods

Neigh-borhood	Commu-nity area	Latina/o/x or Hispanic %	White %	Black %	Housing vacancy %	Below federal poverty line %	18–24 no high school diploma %
Logan Square	22	53.48	35.37	6.68	9.72	21.10	17.62
Humboldt Park	23	52.52	4.92	41.14	16.89	33.95	29.90
East Gar-field Park	27	1.97	3.39	93.11	24.99	44.17	19.97
West Haven	28	3.61	11.22	83.32	18.76	40.95	37.24
North Lawndale	29	5.50	1.85	91.33	26.84	43.76	27.56
Little Village	30	82.13	4.13	13.51	19.42	26.21	51.74
Pilsen	31	81.78	13.73	2.88	18.72	29.66	28.38
Douglas	35	1.86	13.23	77.36	19.71	27.87	7.36
Oakland	36	2.71	3.20	90.96	16.37	34.03	36.34
Grand Boulevard	38	1.11	3.62	93.72	23.00	33.63	21.00
North Kenwood	39	0.62	3.70	90.69	17.58	30.33	6.15
Washing-ton Park	40	1.03	0.15	98.28	26.12	52.59	20.36
Woodlawn	42	1.39	5.04	91.18	26.12	34.54	26.04
South Chicago	46	25.50	1.92	71.61	17.67	30.61	28.85
Chicago Lawn	66	37.22	5.33	55.99	16.64	26.75	26.08
West Engle-wood*	67	1.88	0.75	96.36	22.56	40.48	37.64
Englewood	68	0.40	0.64	98.54	25.78	43.46	32.54
Auburn-Gresham	71	0.80	0.39	98.19	14.35	27.58	29.70

*Not included in the New Communities Program; I include it here because residents of Greater Englewood view it as one neighborhood (Englewood and West Englewood).
Data compiled using census tract information from the 2009 American Community Survey (ACS). As of 2019, only partial census tract information for the 2010 census and 2015 ACS is available.

Drawing on theories of social capital, the Local Initiatives Support Corporation targeted certain community-based organizations to act as "lead agencies" within each neighborhood. These agencies would build a relationship with the corporation, have access to seed grants (ranging from $25,000 to $50,000), network with various city agencies to implement community change, and create resident-informed quality-of-life plans for their respective neighborhoods. With the exception of two nonprofits, they were handpicked by the corporation based on their capacity and their history with each targeted community. Throughout the New Communities Program, according to Local Initiatives Support Corporation senior staff, the organization focused on developing leadership skills within their lead agencies and incorporating lead agency staff into a broader network of nonprofits and city officials. Lead agencies, in turn, focused on building relationships with city officials and other local public and private agencies, in an effort to secure much-needed resources for their communities and better support neighborhood-level initiatives.

Although the sixteen New Communities neighborhoods did see increases in resources, and many of them experienced physical redevelopment initiatives, there was no guarantee that the residents who lived in these communities prior to the New Communities Program would benefit from these changes.

Comprehensive Community Initiatives and Asset-Based Community Development

Operating as an updated comprehensive community initiative (CCI), the New Communities Program reflected broader changes in nonprofit approaches to community development that center on expanding interorganizational networks and attempt to decentralize power. Previous initiatives followed a top-down approach, with experts and urban elites framing development decisions. CCIs aimed to promote community building by supporting and advocating for resident participation, promoting organizational collaboration, and fostering support among community members.[33] In this new model, community-based organizations partnered with national community development intermediaries—which marketed themselves to foundations, municipal governments, and other actors as knowledgeable and capable of successful community redevelopment—to ensure resident representation during the brainstorming phase of redevelopment planning and to fund the agencies and their services.[34] In this way, the New Communities Program incorporated elements of asset-based community development.

Throughout my time in Chicago, I heard asset-based language used by both the New Communities Program affiliates and grassroots organizers; however, differences arose in terms of action and implementation. Extending from the work of Kretzmann and McKnight, asset-based community development identifies the assets, strengths, and resources of a community to work toward addressing community issues. Unlike a clientelistic approach, which promotes (particularly impoverished) resident dependency on external experts to solve complex local issues, the asset-based community development movement involves experts working alongside local community organizations to identify the "gifts, skills, and capacities" of "individuals, associations, and institutions."[35] Once these assets are identified, experts and local groups work together to (1) strengthen ties between residents and organizations and (2) mitigate or solve social injustices.[36]

On the one hand, asset-based community development provides a framework and a model for local activists to battle denigrative narratives and actions by city officials, urban planners, developers, and others who consistently claim that poor neighborhoods lack the capacity, intelligence, or know-how to address ongoing social issues such as poverty, urban decay, violence, and low levels of education. On the other hand, there is a risk that this model will fall into a bootstrap narrative that absolves the state of addressing structural inequities.

Research suggests that partnerships between community nonprofits and development elites often occur at the cost of resident empowerment and community-focused redevelopment.[37] Within the New Communities neighborhoods, some of these costs were incurred, particularly as lead agencies drifted away from their original missions to align more closely with the initiative.

Grassroots Responses to Redevelopment

Despite these challenges, however, grassroots groups used the information gathered by the lead agencies involved in the New Communities Program to expand development opportunities in certain neighborhoods.

This effort was often accomplished through a mix of styles of grassroots organizing and asset-based community development, which focused on both coalition building across communities of color and including and empowering residents at all stages of an action.[38]

One of these styles of organizing was developed by community activist and political theorist Saul Alinsky, who believed in cultivating and empowering local, native leaders as community change agents. With their insider knowledge, he explained, native leaders are better able to understand local concerns and issues. They speak the local language or dialect and may be trusted more easily than an outsider. Another of these styles was developed by Fred Hampton, who spearheaded the Black Panther–led Rainbow Coalition and was raised in Chicago; he believed in coalition building across disenfranchised groups to address larger structural problems, such as poverty and racism. In part as a result of his presence there, the city has a long history of coalition-based community activism within Black and Latina/o/x communities. The ability of such grassroots groups to build bridges across racial, ethnic, and class lines is important to achieving political gains at all levels—not only within Chicago but also nationally.

During the New Communities Program, grassroots groups sometimes sought to accomplish their goals by collaborating with the Local Initiative Support Corporation and the local lead agencies. However, these collaborations nonetheless remained limited and generally occurred only when a partnership was beneficial to the corporation or to the city. In the end, the grassroots initiatives discussed in this book were most successful when groups, using their collective skepticism, engaged in coalition building with internal and external allies.

The Neighborhoods: Little Village and Greater Englewood

In Chicago, the neighborhoods of Little Village and Greater Englewood illustrate the ways that community groups in disenfranchised areas can collaborate with a variety of citywide agencies and national community development intermediaries to engage in resident-led local economic development. If the New Communities Program was meant to increase development initiatives in challenged communities, I wondered what this would mean in two of the most distressed communities in the city. As

TABLE 1.3. 2009 American Community Survey census tract data for Greater Englewood and Little Village as compared to the city of Chicago

2009 American Community Survey	Greater Englewood	Little Village	City of Chicago
Population size	66,159	79,288 (99,288)[a]	2,695,598
% African American	96%	12%	32.90%
% Latina/o/x	1.67%	84%	28.90%
% < high school education	40%	50%	15%
Median income	$22,824	$33,593	$47,371
% unemployed	26.90%	10.80%	9.70%
% below poverty line	33.79%	26.50%	21.40%

a. These are the estimated totals including the undocumented population.

Table 1.3 shows, the demographics in Greater Englewood and Little Village differ vastly from Chicago's 2010 averages.[39] The populations of both neighborhoods have lower-than-average median income and educational attainment and a higher-than-average rate of poverty. Although there are clear similarities between these neighborhoods, differences stem from political history, nonprofit capacity, and racial/ethnic background.

Specifically, Greater Englewood has a sixty-year history of disinvestment, weak and fragmented aldermanic representation (with no aldermanic office; unlike most other areas, the community is divided between six different wards), a significant loss of population, and high levels of empty and abandoned lots and buildings. In contrast, Little Village has a strong small business district, strong political representation (even with low voter turnout rates, and although the neighborhood spans three wards, the majority of residents live in one), and strong ties between local nonprofits and municipal and state politicians. Comparing Little Village and Greater Englewood, therefore, provides an understanding of the ways that external power holders can influence community development in high-poverty areas, despite their differing characteristics.

LITTLE VILLAGE

Located on the near Southwest Side of Chicago, Little Village, or La Villita, is home to the largest Mexican American and immigrant community in the Midwest.[40] Bordering the Cook County Jail, the neighborhood is known across the city as a site of violence, poverty, and overcrowding and, given its location near a major highway and an industrial corridor—with 488.6 acres zoned for industrial use—it's also known for high rates of pollution.[41] This neighborhood is densely populated, although it has experienced some population decline, at −12.94 percent between 2000 and 2010. Despite this density, the neighborhood lacks sufficient green space or public transportation, with limited access to the train system and only two bus lines.[42]

The neighborhood also has an abundance of street activity, higher-than-average traffic, several small businesses, and children playing at all hours in the streets and parks. Local leaders often highlight the neighborhood as the second largest retail strip in the city, amassing sales revenue comparable to the Magnificent Mile, Chicago's high-end downtown shopping district. Little Village's main small business drag extends almost two miles, from Twenty-Sixth and Sacramento to Twenty-Sixth and Kostner (Figure 1.1). Each time I visited the neighborhood, I would walk down this bustling strip, admiring the ethnically and culturally relevant merchandise: everything from books to artwork, clothing, and groceries. Some side streets boast homes with well-manicured yards, flowers, and clean sidewalks. Others reflect urban neglect, with overgrown lots, numerous potholes in the streets, broken and cracked sidewalks, and litter. During the warmer months I would purchase *limonada* and sliced fruit cups with *tajin* chile powder from street vendors, while in the winter I would pick up *tamales de puerco en salsa rojo* and steaming hot *champurrado* on my way to community meetings.

With its prime location near a waterway and two major highways, this historic industrial community houses a number of factories, and in 2018 a new industrial corridor was under construction. The area's industrial history and high density are easy to observe, given the many blue-collar workers (including factory employees, mechanics, and construction workers) and diesel trucks traversing the streets. Little Village also has a history of thriving, capable nonprofit and community groups who provide a variety of services to the local Mexican population. The work of these groups is evident in the maintenance of Twenty-Sixth Street, where flowerpots and ornately designed garbage cans appear on every corner and the streets and sidewalks are mostly clean and neat (Figure 1.2). Several of the organizations I worked with also provided labor rights

Figure 1.1. Small business district and street vendors on Twenty-Sixth Street, Little Village. Photo by Teresa Irene Gonzales, July 5, 2018.

Figure 1.2. Street beautification on Twenty-Sixth Street, Little Village. Photo by Teresa Irene Gonzales, July 5, 2018.

workshops, English language courses, and legal assistance for labor disputes. This community is proudly working-class and proudly Mexican.

GREATER ENGLEWOOD

Eight miles southeast of Little Village is Greater Englewood, a predominantly African American neighborhood consisting of both Englewood and West Englewood.[43] Located on the southeast corridor of the city, Greater Englewood is a predominantly Black community with a population just over sixty-six thousand, a smaller population than that of Little Village. Most residents live in the eastern neighborhood of Englewood rather than West Englewood.

Known within the popular imagination as Chiraq, it is labeled a site of decay, poverty, and extreme violence. Although it was once a booming retail economic center, Greater Englewood has suffered sixty years of city neglect and political disenfranchisement, contributing to high crime, economic decline, low education levels, and concentrated poverty. Within Chicago's city limits, Greater Englewood was hit hardest by the foreclosure crisis and had already experienced decades of real estate fraud.[44] As in many other urban African American communities, beginning in the 1960s Black residents of Greater Englewood contended with inherently racist mortgage lending practices, redlining, and lack of Federal Housing Administration (FHA)–supported mortgages.

These circumstances coupled with the decline of local manufacturing—in particular the closing of Wisconsin Steel and the stockyards in an adjoining neighborhood—and the loss of major retailers and a local hospital have decreased locals' access to jobs and to much-needed amenities. The result was approximately 8,500 abandoned or vacant lots and many streets with only a handful of occupied houses and storefronts (Figure 1.3).[45] In total, Greater Englewood contained 697.6 acres of vacant space. Between 2000 and 2010, the neighborhood witnessed significant population loss (−22.62 percent between 2000 and 2010). After the conclusion of the New Communities Program, between 2013 and 2018, the city shuttered ten public schools in Greater Englewood.

When exploring this community, I was struck by how vacant it seemed compared to the lively street scenes in Little Village. There are few occupied houses, few people on the streets, no street vendors, limited traffic (even at peak rush hour), few kids playing in any of the available

Figure 1.3. Foreclosed and abandoned housing, Greater Englewood. Photo by Teresa Irene Gonzales, July 5, 2018.

parks, few small businesses with storefronts, and no public garbage cans or flowerpots on any of the sidewalk corners (Figure 1.4). What I did notice was the overgrowth of trees, grasses, and other plants and the litter, from broken bottles to old tires, strewn across the numerous abandoned lots. The neighborhood lacks a business district and a local grocery store (however, it does boast an organic farm and weekly market that targets locals, and although it is inaccessible to many Englewood residents, the upscale organic grocery store Whole Foods opened there in September 2016). According to the Local Initiatives Support Corporation officials and others, prior to the New Communities Program the area lacked the nonprofit capacity to deal with such mounting neighborhood issues.[46]

The neighborhood, however, has other assets. Unlike Little Village, Greater Englewood boasts ample public transportation, with access to two train lines (Green and Red) and several bus routes, and it includes five large public parks. The neighborhood is also close to a major highway and is home to Kennedy-King College, one of the seven city colleges in Chicago, and the Washburne Culinary Institute. Furthermore, there is a vibrant arts and underground small business scene. One could

Figure 1.4. Closed and abandoned storefronts, Greater Englewood. Photo by Teresa Irene Gonzales, July 5, 2018.

regularly find slam poet readings, live music, dancing, and open-mic nights at local bars, at community centers, and in vacant lots. Many residents sell items and services from their homes, such as providing child care, doing hair and nails, cooking small-batch meals, baking, creating and selling jewelry, and developing seasonings.

On the surface, the differences between this neighborhood and Little Village are stark. Some of these differences, however, stem from historic racist and classist policies that have systematically ignored and undermined development in Black communities. For example, rather than hire from the neighborhood, local industry often used cheaper migrant and immigrant labor.[47] Additionally, in Englewood machine politics and the neighborhood's fragmentation into six wards have led to multiple failed redevelopment initiatives.

These differences are compounded by the variations in the neighborhoods' elected representation. Chicago is divided into fifty legislative districts called wards, each represented by one elected alderman who serves for four years, with municipal elections in February.[48] Aldermen have a number of powers that include introducing and passing laws, approving budgets and mayoral appointments, and redrawing political boundaries every ten years, after each federal census. They also exercise veto power over development projects in their wards, so although no city code or statute guarantees them this privilege, aldermen have the power to approve or deny any redevelopment initiatives in the communities they represent.[49] This practice has left decisions to local aldermen to the exclusion of residents.[50] In my interviews with nonprofit staff, city officials, neighborhood activists, and the Local Initiatives Support Corporation representatives, I heard consistently that Chicago aldermen were reticent to oppose redevelopment mandates from the mayor's office, regardless of the community's wishes. Even when local residents were opposed, aldermen were not willing to involve themselves in these neighborhood struggles. Such aldermanic representation—or lack thereof—in development decisions has long-lasting impacts on Chicago neighborhoods.

During the period of the New Communities Program (2002–2013), we can see the impact of differing aldermanic representation in both Greater Englewood and Little Village. The boundaries of the Greater Englewood neighborhood overlap with six distinct wards (Table 1.4). Perceived low rates of voter turnout, coupled with the fragmented political boundaries within the neighborhood, and the local aldermen's unwillingness to challenge the mayor's office have resulted in historically mismatched development projects within Greater Englewood. Although the boundaries of Little Village also overlap with several distinct wards (in this case three; Table 1.5), much of Little Village is housed in one distinct ward (the Twenty-Second), with no overlap into adjoining communities. As a result, there is at least one dedicated aldermanic representative for the neighborhood.

Although this better political representation may impact the flow of development dollars into a community, it does not necessarily result in projects that represent or address local needs. As I'll discuss in later chapters, for such projects to occur an active, resident-based civic sector is key.

Despite their differences, Greater Englewood and Little Village overlap in several important ways: they shared narratives regarding violence and criminality commonly associated with Black and Latina/o/x

TABLE 1.4. Ward and aldermanic representation in Greater Englewood 2011

Ward	Alderman
3rd	Pat Dowell[a]
6th	Roderick T. Sawyer[b]
15th	Toni Foulkes[c]
16th	JoAnn Thompson[d]
17th	Latasha Thomas[e]
20th	Willie Cochran[f]

a. Elected in 2007 after defeating incumbent Dorothy Tillman. Tillman was appointed as alderman of the 3rd Ward by Mayor Harold Washington in 1993.
b. Elected in 2011 after defeating incumbent Freddrenna Lyle. Lyle was appointed as alderman of the 6th Ward by Mayor Richard M. Daley in 1998.
c. Elected in 2007.
d. Elected in 2007.
e. Appointed alderman of the 17th Ward by Mayor Richard M. Daley in 2000.
f. Elected 2007.

TABLE 1.5. Ward and aldermanic representation in Little Village 2011

Ward	Alderman
12th	George Cardenas[a]
22nd	Ricardo ("Rick") Muñoz[b]
24th	Michael D. Chandler[c]

a. Elected 2003.
b. Appointed to the 22nd Ward in 1993.
c. Elected 1995 through 2007. Reelected in 2011.

communities, and they also experienced the rise of a strong grassroots sector across each community. Thus, with city hall's plans for redevelopment in these areas, both Little Village and Englewood were included in the New Communities Program.

By analyzing the effects of this program on these two key neighborhoods, I show how powerful national community development intermediaries (like the Local Initiatives Support Corporation) influence local nonprofits and reshape the urban landscape in ways that are not easily seen by local residents. From this work, I identify the intended and unintended consequences of trust and mistrust in urban redevelopment initiatives, which include major tensions between (1) neighborhood and citywide organizations, (2) centralized (top-down) efforts and local input, (3) the city and specific community needs, and (4) organizational mission and on-the-ground practices.

Studying Two Communities

In thinking through my approach to this research, I knew that I wanted to avoid replicating previous studies that had engaged in "poverty pimping," "sympathetic observations," "jungle-book tropes," or "cowboy ethnography."[51] Neither did I wish to engage in what Du Bois terms "car window" (or rather drive-by) sociology, where a researcher simply observes behaviors from a safe, disconnected distance.[52] These approaches risk reifying negative stereotypes of poor, inner-city communities of color as violent, pathological, and in need of intervention. Furthermore, these approaches center the researcher as expert, with little recognition of the ways that individuals are also experts in their everyday lived experiences. These two communities in particular have been overstudied and misrepresented as one-dimensional, both by researchers and by local news outlets. With these concerns in mind, I decided to spend time in both neighborhoods, to familiarize myself with their built environments and local organizations, to understand the ways people collectively used and (re)imagined space, and to observe whether, when, and where development occurred.

This approach required that I first interrogate my own assumptions, fears, biases, and expectations for the research. It would have been much easier for me to focus solely on Latina/o/x communities in Chicago or to research my home neighborhood of Pilsen, especially as it was included in the New Communities Program and I have relationships with several nonprofits there. However, I was concerned that I would be unable to distance myself from research on Pilsen—my family's home for more than sixty years—and I wanted a home base from which I could observe redevelopment at a distance. I also wanted a space to withdraw from the field and consider what I was learning in Greater Englewood and Little Village. At home in Pilsen, I could check in about my research with friends at nonprofit and grassroots organizations. For these reasons, I decided to remove Pilsen from my study and instead established a cross-racial comparison of the two most "distressed" communities in the initiative.

Knowing that urban redevelopment affects groups differently, I sensed that there was a deeper story of redevelopment in Black and Mexican Chicago. Uneven (re)development affects both Latina/o/x and Black communities in the city, yet so many studies of Chicago have focused on one racial and/or ethnic group in isolation. Although many people do stay in their neighborhoods and continue to live their lives there, many others move elsewhere. Additionally, people, ideas, and policies travel via city-level processes and community activism. By comparing two neighborhoods, I sought to identify both differences and commonalities that might explain broader patterns of redevelopment.

During the first year of the study, I spent time walking through both neighborhoods, taking notes on the built environment, exploring redevelopment initiatives, and observing how, when, and in what capacity groups worked (or didn't work) together. Admittedly, I was more comfortable walking through Little Village. It is a familiar neighborhood; my immediate family had lived there when I was born, and because it is adjacent to Pilsen, I had often walked there to visit friends. My mom is a retired teacher from a Little Village grammar school, and I have provided workshops to area students on community efforts and student-led research. As a multiracial Mexican American, I could easily navigate Little Village without significant visual markers of difference. Greater Englewood, in contrast, was initially a daunting place for me to visit regularly, as I had to confront my own media-driven fears regarding the neighborhood.

Still, the Pilsen of my childhood was in some ways similar to Greater Englewood. Although it is gentrifying, Pilsen has struggled with urban decay, overpolicing, negative stereotypes, rampant gang violence, and aldermanic neglect and corruption. Growing up, I experienced my own share of interpersonal and state violence, and I was often frustrated by the overwhelmingly bad publicity that my own neighborhood received. I also painfully understood the ways this image had affected people's perceptions of me. As various scholars of urban poverty remind us, people and the spaces they inhabit can become synonymous in popular perception. The places where we grow up and live thus have the power to frame our public identities.

Even with this history in mind, however, I was not immune to fear in Greater Englewood. Well aware of the negativity the neighborhood had long endured, I initially made sure that my family knew where I was going when I set out for the area. Instead of taking public transportation (even though I hate driving), I borrowed a car and made sure to park on well-lit streets. These were not precautions I took when traveling to Little Village, a neighborhood also known for high rates of violence. My fear of Greater Englewood stemmed in part from traveling to an unfamiliar community, but as a Chicago native, I also knew and was influenced by the neighborhood's broader reputation for extreme violence.

Only after working with residents in Greater Englewood did my fears and biases begin to dissipate. After a few months of data collection, I recognized that both its residents and its nonprofit and grassroots organizations were contending with many of the same challenges I observed in Little Village. These included news media representations of crime and decay and regimes of political neglect and state-led violence that had led to closed schools, lack of public services, and predatory lending practices. Because of political districting and city hall's extensive neglect of Black neighborhoods, however, Greater Englewood contended with even deeper issues of urban disenfranchisement. Neighborhood problems are evident in the lack of physical and economic development, from abandoned buildings to empty storefronts and a lack of street traffic or children playing outside. Few eyes watch the streets in Greater Englewood.

As I worked with groups in both neighborhoods, I realized that residents and community organizers were applying collective skepticism in their dealings with me, even though they approached that collective skepticism in different ways. Throughout my time in the field, people were willing to speak with me, but those I encountered in Greater Englewood were more welcoming and responsive than those in Little Village. Initially, this difference surprised me—after all, I thought, I am a racial insider in Little Village. Yet during conversations in Little Village, some people asked why I was not studying my own neighborhood. Articulating suspicion and frustration with researchers who studied "others," they advocated for studying one's own. In contrast, I heard none of this concern in Greater Englewood. Instead, people there acknowledged the fear about the neighborhood, particularly at night. When I discussed my own initial fears, I was met with comments like "You're safer here than in other places; people think you're White and [therefore] important. Black people on the other hand, aren't safe. We're more likely to experience violence in Greater Englewood than anybody else." I heard this statement often, and it shed light on the different levels of openness I experienced in these communities during my fieldwork.

Method

To better understand collective responses to urban redevelopment and to ensure that I built collaborative relationships with groups in these neighborhoods, I conducted a two-year ethnographic study of Greater Englewood and Little Village between 2011 and 2013. Drawing on feminist theories of reciprocity in research, I became an active member of six organizations.[53] These included the lead agencies identified by the New Communities Program and, in each neighborhood, an additional two community organizations working with a lead agency on more than one project. During my tenure in Chicago, I attended community and town hall meetings held by city offices regarding development, organizational events, and information sessions. Throughout, I sought to identify the processes through which various organizational actors attempted to include residents in neighborhood decisions. Between 2012 and 2016, I returned to Chicago and supplemented my initial observations by attending additional meetings and community events.

I also conducted forty-five semistructured, in-depth interviews with key individuals in a range of organizations. Among these informants were members of lead agencies across six neighborhoods; staff from various city and statewide departments; program officers associated with the New Communities Program and the Local Initiatives Support Corporation; former employees of both the Local Initiatives Support Corporation and lead agencies; members of comparable nonlead agencies, including both community-based and grassroots organizations in these neighborhoods; residents; and journalists who had been covering these areas of the city and documenting their redevelopment. To protect the identity of individuals, I use pseudonyms throughout. I use real names only when discussing quotes from newspaper articles and public comments made by local politicians or when identifying artists and founding members of organizations. For verification purposes, I have not changed the names of any of the organizations, neighborhoods, or streets discussed.

Outline of This Book

Throughout the book, I showcase the various ways that Black and Latina/o/x residents strategically engage trust and collective skepticism to influence redevelopment in their neighborhoods. Chapter 2 describes the New Communities Program as it sought to create a common culture, using particular language regarding development in the target neighborhoods. The Local Initiatives Support Corporation staff built deep relationships of trust between their partner lead agencies and powerful city elites who could steer resources into these communities. As indicated earlier, although these partnerships did infuse money and technical expertise into the targeted neighborhoods, they also restricted advocacy and controversial development projects. As a senior staff member highlighted, much of the New Communities Program centered on "more the people of a place and less the physicality of a place." This focus was evident in the programming that lead agencies provided, such as after-school programs, workforce development, and peace initiatives. Such activities can broaden the skill sets of residents, but they did little to mitigate the lack of opportunity for marginalized populations. Applying the discourse of professionalization and policy neutrality, I argue, these trust networks socialized members into a single organizational culture—one that focuses on remedying the shortcomings of individuals—at a cost to local neighborhoods.

Chapter 3 extends this argument to look at complementary aspects of trust and mistrust in community development. I analyze the tactics, strategies, and programming practices implemented by two distinct types of community groups: nonprofit lead agencies and grassroots organizations. Whereas the lead agencies focused on the goals of the New Communities Program, including social service provision and relationship building, the grassroots organizations combined community development practices with community organizing to expand local development and increase the leadership skills of residents. These processes highlight the growing divide between formal development policies, aimed to transform the individual, and local responses, aimed to transform structural inequities while also developing local leadership potential.

By tracing coalition building among grassroots community organizations, chapter 4 identifies the high level of mistrust among the lead agencies, the intermediary, and grassroots groups unaffiliated with the New Communities Program. Still, this chapter explains, these organizations collaborated and shared ideas, resources, and information. Goal-focused collaborative relationships—what I term networks of opportunity—provided benefits to both local residents and community organizations, but rather than working toward building trust, grassroots groups in these networks used their collective skepticism of the New Communities Program, the lead agencies, local politicians, and other external organizations as a tool to ensure a more careful evaluation of what they could accomplish. They thus assessed the information they shared with a more critical eye toward project outcomes.

Because of their collective skepticism, grassroots groups actively searched for collaborative relationships with supportive groups across both the city and the nation. As this chapter explains, such an approach to networking, while potentially difficult and time-consuming, allows organizations to connect their local causes to broader national issues and is particularly useful in networks that contain unequal power relations. Furthermore, where organizational members are open to public questioning of these projects' potential consequences, networks of opportunity and resident-focused leadership development can more readily allow heterogeneous approaches to community development. As a result, powerful politicians, intermediaries, and community developers are unable to steer growth by way of consensus. Within Greater Englewood and Little Village, these two unique approaches included *partnering with local agencies* and *partnering with a broad network*.

In the concluding chapter I consider the value of trust and suggest new ways to engage residents and improve resident-led inclusion at all levels of redevelopment: research, planning, implementation, and assessment of results. I begin with a discussion of the Local Initiatives Support Corporation's model of "comprehensive community development." Despite the feel-good nature embedded in ideas of trust, evidence suggests that the corporation's approach may actually continue a history of socially unjust urban development, with its documented inequities. As feminist scholars have highlighted, collective decision making can conceal the various ways that power manifests itself.[54] This chapter explores this concept and explains how trust in combination with mistrust can yield more equitable results.

2

A Seat at the Table

The New Communities Program, Organizational Relationships, and Socialization into Community Development

We have to move from a poverty ghetto to a choice community.
—Executive director of a New Communities Program lead agency, 2012

It's great that individuals are trying to do block club work or very modest work, but they don't have the actual infrastructure of a nonprofit to be able to do anything long-term.
—Querida Villanueva, 2013

There should be no such thing as a lead agency, it doesn't promote coalition building.
—Quad Communities organizer, 2017

On a warm fall day in 2012, I sat down with Marta Rodriguez over coffee at a locally owned café. A lifelong resident of a predominantly Mexican community in Chicago, Marta had recently left her senior position with one of the sixteen lead agencies in Chicago's New Communities Program. As mentioned earlier, following the trend of collaborative public-private partnerships, the city had partnered with the Local Initiatives Support Corporation, the MacArthur Foundation, and designated neighborhood nonprofits (referred to as lead agencies) to do this work.[1] Through her engagement with it, Marta noted both positive and negative outcomes of the redevelopment initiative.

In our conversation about her perceptions of redevelopment in the neighborhood, Marta was mostly positive about the role of the New Communities Program in growing the lead agency and in bringing resources to the community. She believed in the lead agency and its mission. Using language that echoed that of staff at the Local Initiatives Support Corporation, she highlighted the importance of organizational cooperation that included "multidimensional comprehensive community development . . . that's not just bricks and mortar, but also green space . . . using local assets." However, after nine years with the New Communities Program, she was skeptical that the initiative could create meaningful, lasting change in the lives of residents. Ultimately, she became disillusioned with nonprofit work.

When I asked Marta to elaborate, her answer surprised me: The lead agency had benefitted greatly from its relationship to the Local Initiatives Support Corporation, she explained, but the direction of the nonprofit had changed. It had always been a conflict-oriented organization that directly challenged local politicians' decisions and was committed to redressing deep, structural inequities for area residents. Now, however, the lead agency focused less on the "root causes" of inequality and more on surface-level programming that focused on the individual. Although Marta recognized the added benefits of working with, rather than against, the city, she decried the shift in the agency's development initiatives, away from the concerns of poor residents of color.

Across Chicago, other residents and lead agency staff echoed this skepticism. To achieve their goals and attract much-needed resources to their communities, the city's community-based organizations engaged in a variety of relationships to attract investors and build coalitions as the basis for collaboration.[2] To negotiate with funders and politicians regarding neighborhood needs, they worked to build an organized, if not always unified, front. Like organizations across the country, however, Chicago's nonprofits faced decreasing funding and an increasing array of quantifiable measures of accountability. These imperatives had come to shape a process that could elide community needs.[3]

My conversation with Marta also highlights another national trend: one in which city officials partner with organizations like the Local Initiatives Support Corporation and community-based organizations to incorporate residents' ideas into citywide (re)development plans. These partnerships seem like they will benefit the residents but often have negative effects. In Chicago, the New Communities Program overwhelmingly focused on building deep networks of trust between partner agencies and the city. On the one hand, such networks of trust can socialize organizations into a community development culture where all parties "speak the same language" and work toward similar goals. Networks of trust also increase accountability and opportunities and ensure that members of community organizations are considered for grants and are privy to sensitive information. On the other hand, these networks can hide power imbalances, shield member agencies from scandal and criticism, and set an area's development agenda, particularly where member agencies are strongly embedded in elite network relations. As a result, organizations may find that funding and prestige are closely tied to their adherence to the network's cultural norms—which often extend rather than mitigate marginalization for low-income communities of color.[4] Focusing on the pitfalls of trust—the central theme of this chapter—we are able to uncover its insidious nature in replicating inequity.

The New Communities Program fits squarely into this trend. It expanded interorganizational networks of trust to ensure resident representation and fund local agencies and their services, but these changes came at the cost of resident empowerment and community-led redevelopment.[5] My interactions with Marta and with officials at the Local Initiatives Support Corporation indicated the process underlying this disempowerment: these partnerships socialized community groups, encouraging those involved to trust in city officials, technocrats, and local development experts rather than maintaining the skepticism they needed to challenge deep inequities. Likewise, neighborhood nonprofits thus learned to trust that the Local Initiatives Support Corporation had the funds, knowledge, and expertise to implement resident-led redevelopment instead of staying connected with their own perspective. National development intermediaries like the Local Initiatives Support Corporation, however, do not always prioritize community needs—they are themselves nonprofits, beholden to funders and local politicians, and they have their own redevelopment goals.

During my time in Chicago, I was struck by the Local Initiatives Support Corporation's attempts to contribute to this shift by facilitating trust between organizations and building a reputation for expertise in community development. Their staff believed that trust could promote community partnerships and redevelopment, and their approach to community development invested much time and money in creating the conditions for interorganizational coalitions. As a result, in Little Village and Greater Englewood, trust and collective skepticism—a tactical tool that draws on the expertise of community organizers, centers histories of dispossession, and requires elites to explicitly outline their efforts to include and support low-income residents of color—circulated within a network that linked actors in an organizational field that included philanthropy, city hall, local community groups, and oftentimes residents.[6] Organizational *trust*, however, was not evenly distributed within the networks the Local Initiatives Support Corporation tried to foster; instead, it reflected inequity in organizational power that, I came to realize, was sustained by design. This uneven distribution of trust had consequences for the lead agencies in Little Village and Greater Englewood and for the kinds of work they could do.

The Local Initiatives Support Corporation's New Communities Program: Model and Network

Although the New Communities Program was primarily a (re)development initiative, it focused on creating and maintaining deep relationships of trust to ensure that partner organizations were open to both working with elite partners and modifying their internal cultures and practices. In fact, senior staff at the Local Initiatives Support Corporation highlighted the combination of their unifying method, networking approach, and process of socialization as a selling point of the New Communities Program. These elements, however, had different impacts in different neighborhoods, depending on how fully each neighborhood nonprofit embraced the approach. Those that wholly embraced it benefitted greatly—for them, alignment with the program's goals increased clout, resources, and political interest in both the nonprofit and the neighborhood. Not all lead agencies, however, successfully implemented the program or built relationships of trust with city agencies or local residents, and those that did not benefitted far less from the program or even incurred new costs.

The Local Initiatives Support Corporation model was particularly successful in Little Village, where the lead agency, Enlace, moved away from its previous conflict-oriented practices (e.g., marches, sit-ins, hunger strikes), which challenged the root causes of injustice, toward more traditional development efforts, which focused on individual behaviors and left the preexisting power structures in place. In contrast, the Englewood lead agency, Teamwork Englewood, adhered less rigorously to the New Communities Program model and was less successful by the standards of the initiative. It struggled to realize the initiative's goals and was often in conflict with both the Local Initiatives Support Corporation staff and neighborhood residents. Although the agency's executive board did acknowledge the benefits of the corporation and attempted to align with its approach to community development, its organizers were frustrated with the limits on their ability to create deep social change and thus questioned whether an outside agency could truly represent the needs of Greater Englewood residents.

Scholars have highlighted that resource scarcity may compel local nonprofits, particularly more activist-oriented organizations, to adopt less confrontational tactics.[7] As will be discussed later, this combined with the opportunity to connect with political, economic, and foundation elites created an environment where more mainstream approaches to social change were valued.[8] This approach created challenges for residents and community groups who yearned for structural changes to inequality.

The New Communities Program as Redevelopment

Conventional models of local economic development rely on a combination of development experts and government officials to address specific issues, such as housing or industry. Recent advancements in development, however, call for the inclusion of local residents at specific stages—usually the design phase—of new projects.[9] In the United States, local economic development usually takes a place-based approach to development that emphasizes development activities in and by cities, districts, and regions. These plans receive funding from and are often managed by local and national governmental and philanthropic organizations. Local community-based organizations work with external agencies to promote economic development within their respective neighborhoods through, for example, an affordable housing initiative, the (re)vitalization of a business district, workforce development, or the creation of an industrial corridor.[10]

The dilemma for local nonprofits that hope to engage in this process is that city officials often support development strategies that overly rely on growth rather than on comprehensive development;[11] that is, they emphasize such strategies as an increase in land values, the development of a business district, beautification efforts, and the attraction of corporate investors.[12] Unless there are mechanisms in place for holding commercial and residential real estate rates constant when using such a growth-focused development strategy, real estate taxes and, in turn, rents and leases may increase, thus paving the way for gentrification and/or displacement to occur.

Although the New Communities Program was an extension of local economic development models, it was cognizant of the potential pitfalls of development on marginalized residents. Thus, it worked to improve conditions in low-income areas through a seemingly holistic approach that was strategic, targeted, and comprehensive: it sought input through community visioning.[13] Resident input and community visioning are not new to development—planners have used these tactics since the 1980s—but a high level of resident involvement at the planning phase marked the program's strategy for building relationships of trust among local organizations and, in each neighborhood, between residents and lead agencies.[14]

As staff from the Local Initiatives Support Corporation and the lead agencies explained, two major components of the New Communities Program were its dual focus on relationship building and resident-inspired (re)development. The ten-year process included identifying and recruiting relevant, community-based nonprofits with strong records of community organizing. These lead agencies were then invited into the program's process and trained in the Local Initiatives Support Corporation's model of community (re)development, which included help in creating blueprints for physical and human redevelopment. As Querida Villanueva, a senior staff member at the corporation, stated matter-of-factly, "We don't invite anyone in; we want a lead agency who will convene partners, will go through a comprehensive planning process so that they have a blueprint that says here's the vision for the neighborhood, here's what we want to do. It's the methodology, core engagement, planning, communication, action. That's our shorthand for it, so that people know what we mean."

Figure 2.1. Cover of Englewood quality-of-life plan.

How did this comprehensive planning process work in practice? The initial phase of the New Communities Program, launched in 2002, centered on the creation of resident-informed quality-of-life plans in each neighborhood. To create the plans, lead agencies conducted town hall meetings with residents over twelve to twenty-four months. During these meetings, staff from the lead agencies used community visioning techniques, dividing attendees into small groups and asking them to indicate, through drawings and phrases, their ideas, hopes, and plans for the neighborhood's future. After a short discussion in small groups, representatives presented their ideas to the larger group. Lead agency staff then collected these ideas and used them to inform the final quality-of-life plans. With some variation, community visioning meetings were repeated across each neighborhood several times.

In Englewood, the resulting plan, titled "Englewood: Making a Difference" (Figure 2.1), drew from the input of 650 residents and 20 leaders of community organizations in town hall meetings held between June 2004

Figure 2.2. Example of a community event in Greater Englewood. Photo by Roberto Medina, October 21, 2012.

and June 2005 (Figure 2.2). The plan called for ten specific strategies for targeted redevelopment: attracting new industries that would provide living-wage jobs, improving abandoned and public spaces, rebuilding retail spaces, creating mixed-income housing, promoting healthy living through diet and exercise, improving safety, improving academic performance, creating opportunities for civic engagement, addressing populations with special needs, and creating a community network.[15] In Little Village, between May 2003 and December 2004, planning engaged approximately 100 residents and 35 leaders of community organizations. This plan, titled "Little Village: Capital of the Mexican Midwest" (Figure 2.3), encompassed forty projects, including those focused on healthy families, high-quality education, an improved business district, maintenance of existing housing, parks and improvements to green spaces, safety and peace in the community, expanded opportunities for the arts, and sustainable and environmentally friendly industry and jobs.[16]

Figure 2.3. Cover of Little Village quality-of-life plan.

This process of community engagement served three goals. First, it captured residents' visions for the future of their neighborhood while also outlining a path toward achieving particular goals. Second, it served as an initial step in socializing lead agencies into the Local Initiatives Support Corporation's model of community (re)development, as lead agency staff used the model and rhetoric of community engagement and upheld the New Communities Program's goals for resident-inspired redevelopment. And third, it laid the groundwork for building hierarchical trust relationships among residents, lead agencies, and city hall. Community meetings compelled residents to reimagine their neighborhoods creatively and interactively, and many residents believed that they had substantial input in development decisions.

Such inclusive planning can also, of course, present residents with the perception of community engagement while moving forward with a political and economic agenda that does not actually account for resident concerns. For the Local Initiatives Support Corporation, the approach had additional benefits: this sharing of resources among city agencies, local nonprofits, and the New Communities Program allowed the intermediary to remain well connected to both local agencies and city officials and to demonstrate clear achievements for the program's social services, interorganizational collaboration, and large-scale resident involvement in planning. The result thus showcased the corporation's expertise in community redevelopment, regardless of whether it truly served the interests of the local community.

In addition to presenting the city with a model for successfully gathering resident feedback, even if that feedback was not necessarily used, the program also provided the city with information on each neighborhood's current land use, potential for land use, and ideas for future large-scale development. Despite the fact that the Local Initiatives Support Corporation was primarily lauded for its approach to community development through the expansion of social services in poor communities, its work on these physical development projects and human development programming also provided elected officials and public agencies with easily recognizable wins.[17]

Given its own goals, in its work with community-based agencies, the Local Initiatives Support Corporation filtered input through its strategies and guidelines for development; as a result, it may have challenged community organizations that had their own preferred projects. For example, the corporation withdrew from contentious development projects, such as the development of a park, and replaced lead agencies that failed to meet its expectations. Such maneuvers may lead to more effective organizations, with more clearly defined and executed development strategies, but they may also divorce programming from community-based needs. These intended and unintended consequences highlight the role of development intermediaries in framing the ways that community nonprofits address social issues in low-income areas. They also raise questions regarding local input into revitalizing neighborhoods and the power of community-based organizations in representing the needs of neighborhood residents.[18]

Socialization into a Common Development Culture

I was surprised to learn that one of the key goals of the New Communities Program was to socialize its members into a common organizational culture and development method. I tried to figure out what, exactly, that process meant—how, for example, might that goal play out in particular interactions? From senior officials at the Local Initiatives Support Corporation and the lead agencies, I learned that socialization was directly linked to the program's position on community development. As these officials explained, the project was framed by the corporation's broader goal to change community redevelopment in Chicago by increasing intraneighborhood collaboration and networking across agencies in the city, community, and private and philanthropic sectors.[19] In the words of Nereyda Smith, a corporation staff member, "The foundation of our work is to set a vision for a *new* neighborhood and the multiple strategies it will take to get there. That's the framework that we work in" (emphasis added).

To achieve these goals, the Local Initiatives Support Corporation promoted intraneighborhood meetings, aiming to engender trust among members of lead agencies and to socialize them into the New Communities Program model. Neighborhood meetings promoted a professional culture of community development, principally through workshops and trainings. They were convened, under the aegis of the program, first during the planning phases for neighborhood quality of life and then through monthly meetings with the Local Initiatives Support Corporation staff. Focusing on establishing and expanding networks to support development, the corporation thus connected community organizations with the city's political and economic elites.

The Local Initiatives Support Corporation facilitated changes to community development by convening an intentional network of nonprofit leaders—it included executive directors from over fifty community-based organizations as well as corporation representatives. Members met every other month to share practices, network with other executive directors, and receive updates from the corporation. Participation in this network allowed community representatives to brainstorm about common issues, build informal networks, and, in some cases, collaborate on initiatives.[20] At the same time, this network provided lead agencies with ongoing access to the Local Initiatives Support Corporation's relationships with private entities, philanthropic agencies, and city officials and departments. Access to both the network and a shared culture allowed the New Communities Program to institutionalize a specific development process throughout the city. The commonality it created ensured that there would be a common framing for larger conversations regarding development and relationships of trust and maintained the program's approach and methodology across all neighborhoods (and potentially across all sites nationally).

After a year and a half of observing participants in Greater Englewood and Little Village, I sat with Nereyda Smith and Betsy West, two senior Local Initiatives Support Corporation officials, in their downtown office. Centrally located in a modern, almost sterile building in Chicago's financial district, the office was bustling with activity. Several staff and executive directors of lead agencies in the New Communities Program were present for a monthly meeting, conversing in the hallways over coffee and pastries. As I entered the small conference room, I saw several familiar faces from Greater Englewood and Little Village. I smiled in greeting, but these usually friendly organizers nervously walked past and glanced sideways at Betsy and Nereyda.[21]

During our conversation, I listened as Nereyda highlighted the importance of the New Communities Program network and its shared culture. For her, relationships were key: "The New Communities Program was a massive, amazing demonstration of a particular model that included two full-time staff, some overhead, and seed dollars to advance a quality-of-life plan. A small portfolio for program officers—which meant they got to go *deep* and build *deep* relationships. A lot of money into human capital to build *deep relationships of trust* and move seed dollars out the door. . . . A lot of great work happened, and *a lot of great relationships were built*" (emphasis added). Nereyda further highlighted the program's innovative processes. Despite external criticism of the Local Initiatives Support Corporation's funders and outside consultants, Nereyda and others were convinced that the model remained the best option for urban development:

> The New Communities Program was also a methodology and a framework that taught us how to do this kind of work, which now we know how to do. And *build the relationships of trust* and have a track record of getting things done, which we did.
>
> We demonstrated; we learned; we're moving forward . . . people want to get things done in neighborhoods. *Especially our neighborhoods*—no one knows how to do it. We know how to do it.

Whether it's right or wrong with our lead agency structure, that's how we operate. *And the good ones know how to tap into their partners and give them these other opportunities. . . .*

The network will continue for as long as the lead agencies are interested in participating. . . . *This network provides our partner organizations with a shared language and culture, [and] this is really, really critical. A big part of what we [the Local Initiatives Support Corporation] do is build a common culture, language, and a common framework.* (emphasis added)

For Nereyda and others at the corporation, the "good" lead agencies, like the one in Little Village, embraced relationship building, situated themselves as neighborhood intermediaries, aligned their goals with those of the New Communities Program, and worked with (rather than against) their allies in the network.

Given the Local Initiatives Support Corporation's focus on building relationships through socialization, the growth of its network could be claimed as a measure of success. But such claims often proved problematic: with its lead agencies operating as local intermediaries, the corporation could expand opportunities to other neighborhood groups and thereby claim—often inaccurately—the successes of any local nonprofits it deemed "good" at collaborating and coalition building. As a result, any successful projects in a neighborhood served by the New Communities Program—regardless of who facilitated the process—could be touted as a success for the Local Initiatives Support Corporation. In separate conversations I had with nonprofit staff across six of the New Communities neighborhoods, each person highlighted this issue. For instance, when asked about the kinds of support that his organization received from partnering with the neighborhood lead agency, Steven Santos, the executive director of a nonprofit focused on housing and citizenship in predominantly Latina/o/x communities, angrily commented, "We received no support—no money, no staff, no technical training, nothing—for our work. But, the [lead agency] claims our programming as a successful example of the [New Communities] initiative. We were doing this work before LISC [the Local Initiatives Support Corporation arrived], and we'll be doing this work when they leave."[22]

Trust as a Political Tool

As I thought through the impact of building trust and social capital as urban development policy, my extended conversation with Nereyda Smith and Betsy West was key. Over the next two hours, both women were at times candid and at other times guarded. As a young Latina who had grown up in one of the New Communities Program neighborhoods and had gone on to do graduate work at the University of California, Berkeley, I sensed from them a mix of pride, a desire to help, and suspicion of me and my work. I had grown accustomed to this response to my inquiries and often used my youth, gender, ethnic background, and personal connections to ease my informants' suspicions. As in other cases, with Betsy and Nereyda I was both an insider (given our gender or ethnoracial similarities) and an outsider (as a researcher). Yet true to their focus on relationship building, these Local Initiatives Support Corporation executives saw me as a potential ally and engaged in a much franker conversation than I had anticipated.

At one point Betsy asked why I had waited so long to speak with staff at the Local Initiatives Support Corporation and why I was not solely interviewing executive directors of nonprofits. Playfully, she asked whether I was searching for "the real story." My uncomfortable response to the second question was a mix of yes and no. I explained that I wanted to build rapport with neighborhood residents, activists, and nonprofit staff, to understand the New Communities Program from a variety of perspectives. Interspersing my questions with their own, Nereyda and Betsy seemed to be trying to gauge my response to the program. Each time I explained my understanding of its processes, they would respond with "good job" or "smart girl." Although some of their questions made me uncomfortable, I came to realize that Nereyda and Betsy were simultaneously providing me with information and reinforcing my subordinate position as a student and a "young" person (albeit one well into her thirties).

My conversation with Nereyda and Betsy clarified both the benefits and the constraints of economic development in Chicago. Nereyda highlighted the lack of aldermanic accountability in some neighborhoods and explained that their aldermen could easily claim ignorance regarding redevelopment initiatives. In Nereyda's and Betsy's view, this lack of local representation fueled resident frustration. When I asked how this arrangement could possibly benefit local aldermen—who are elected officials—both women noted the power of the mayor's office. Chicago's patronage politics, their accounts revealed, pervaded the New Communities Program, both under Mayor Richard M. Daley and under Mayor Rahm Emanuel. This approach to city politics provided benefits to aldermen who supported the mayor's office in all decisions.

The impact of machine politics on redevelopment decisions had come up several times during interviews, public meetings, and casual conversations. As one respondent in Greater Englewood had noted, "The elected officials, they're the ones who have the power . . . the community is really controlled by the city and by the aldermanic representatives."[23] Another respondent from the Quad Communities had similarly commented, "You can't get anything done in Chicago unless you go the political route."[24] Yet another had noted, "I could have all the ideas in the world, but if I don't get that buy-in at the very beginning from the elected officials, it's just not going anywhere."[25] Scholars have similarly highlighted the effects of machine politics on nonprofits, urban development, and poverty eradication.[26]

How, then, did Chicago politics, with local power centralized in the hands of elected officials, affect the New Communities Program? What political forces shaped how community groups agitated for redistributive projects? How, in turn, did city politics inform residents' collective skepticism of neighborhood initiatives? In Chicago, the city's expectation of top-down trust extended to the program. Whereas the Local Initiatives Support Corporation focused on maintaining friendly relationships, the city maintained control of the program, reinforcing residents' experience of exclusion and undermining reciprocal trust in processes of redevelopment.

Constraints to Relationship Building

As they told me more about Chicago's patronage politics, Nereyda and Betsy emphasized the need for trust. Both identified social services and relationship building as essential elements in the New Communities process. Nereyda stated, "All we invest in is community organizations and their human development work." In response, I noted issues raised by community activists and asked about funders' constraints. Betsy rolled her eyes and replied, "At the end of the day, philanthropy and the state really have the final say on what programs are funded, regardless of how effective the program is." I asked for an example, and they elaborated:

> BETSY: Community change and quantifiable change is possible; it just takes a lot of money, a lot of sophistication by the intermediary and local partners, and a lot of attention to paying for the research.
>
> NEREYDA: For example, the tech-focused program Smart Communities, it literally in two years' time, with federal stimulus dollars, with a coordinated approach, led to 15 percent broadband usage among residents above and beyond what the normal trajectory was for other similar neighborhoods.
>
> BETSY: This was a $9 million program over two years in five neighborhoods; that's a lot of money. MacArthur put in $600K just for research. We got to quantifiable community change, and the funding still went away.
>
> NEREYDA: The intervention still stopped.

I began to ask why the funding stopped, but Nereyda interjected that the program was no longer in line with development goals for Chicago. Rather than support a program with clear benefits to area residents, funders and the city decided to move on and fund other, new ideas.

During my time in Chicago, many people cited such a lack of sustained funds to support effective urban programming as a significant problem. Their concern highlights constraints that external forces impose on all nonprofits, from community-based organizations to large-scale national redevelopment intermediaries. These constraints result in tensions between urban elites' plans for the city and residents' hopes, dreams, and visions for their neighborhoods. For example, despite the 15 percent increase in bandwidth usage that Nereyda cited, the project ultimately failed to gain sustainable funding.

Much of what I learned during my two hours with Betsy and Nereyda affirmed what I had seen on the streets of Chicago and heard from community members. However, my interview with them also enhanced my understanding of the ways in which intermediaries in national community development have framed local economic development policy. The approach is streamlined; draws extensively on scholarly research; focuses on modernizing underdeveloped, impoverished, and racialized areas; and embraces a business model of efficiency and replication. In developing a single model of redevelopment for low-income communities of color, the Local Initiatives Support Corporation demonstrated its expertise in redevelopment to city elites and promoted trust in its vision for planning. This model could then be applied to different regions.

Trust, Not Advocacy

Although the New Communities Program aimed to address the historical exclusion of poor residents from large-scale redevelopment initiatives, the Local Initiatives Support Corporation's stance as a development intermediary prevented it from engaging in, or supporting, advocacy that could lead to substantive policy changes or even to resident-led community development. Instead, to ensure that the program and its personnel maintained friendly relations with powerful political, economic, and institutional actors, the corporation worked to enhance trust with city officials and required the same commitment from lead agencies affiliated with the New Communities Program in its target communities. As a result, the program seems to have done more to support its own existence than it did to benefit the communities in the long run.

As mentioned earlier, integration into the New Communities Program's culture ensured that lead agencies moved away from advocacy that could address structural inequities because it might jeopardize relationships with political and economic leaders. Therefore, although they advocated for a holistic approach to development, the Local Initiatives Support Corporation typically supported conventional programming such as affordable housing (i.e., affordability aligned with the median income of the county rather than of the neighborhood) or social services like workforce training, peace initiatives, and educational programs for youth and adults. These forms of community development typically do not push the boundaries of existing policies but rather seek efficient implementation and resources for partner communities.

In fact, the New Communities Program focused exclusively on these kinds of programs and on coalition building—contrary to the understanding of many residents and local nonprofits, they never promoted advocacy. The Local Initiatives Support Corporation members believed that advocacy for policy change could undermine relationships of trust, which staff had worked so hard to build, both with the city and with their funders. Staff members noted a number of rationales for placing trust over advocacy. "The bulk of what we do is focused on better schools, safer streets, jobs for youth and adults, activities for youth," I was told, and "[we try to] be a resource and be valuable to policy makers and to funders and to city officials. . . . We never try to surprise our friends in the public sector or in the foundation sector." As another staff member made clear, "We've never been an advocacy organization . . . we're not out to change the world. We work with others who are trying to change the world, and we collaborate with them in a variety of ways, but that's not us."[27]

The New Communities Program thus gathered residents for their input—which included living-wage jobs, expanded social services, and physical projects such as parks and affordable housing—but implemented these initiatives only when they aligned with broader citywide goals for redevelopment. Nikki Song, executive director of a Southwest Side lead agency, cautiously explained that the Local Initiatives Support Corporation limited her organization's freedom to respond to unique local needs and pressured it to focus on easily implemented beautification projects rather than on more relevant issues. Indeed, the corporation had notified lead agencies that the mayor, city administration, and certain city departments opposed some of the initiatives highlighted in the quality-of-life plans.[28]

For instance, as will be discussed further in chapter 4, at the behest of city officials the Local Initiatives Support Corporation would not support the creation of a park in Little Village, even though residents had made it a priority in the quality-of-life report. According to a corporation staff member, "It was pretty clear that [Mayor Daley] and the Park District and the city administration were foursquare against [the park]." When Little Village's lead agency approached the Local Initiatives Support Corporation for help with the project, the organization was told, "We can't solve that for you. We can help you build your organization, and you can organize. But you also have to understand that there's a cost to [focusing on the park]."[29] The organization understood that advocating for the park meant jeopardizing their access to city officials, funding, and political clout, which in turn could threaten future projects. To ensure that they remained friendly with the corporation and city hall, the lead agency transferred the project to an organization unaffiliated with the New Communities Program.

Similarly, my interviews with city officials and my observations at community meetings highlighted the Local Initiatives Support Corporation's refusal to challenge city-led initiatives. The intermediary avoided activities that might be controversial or damaging to relationships with city officials. Local nonprofit staff and residents expressed deep frustration with the corporation for its unwillingness to support local agencies and challenge city officials on certain development initiatives. Note, however, that although the corporation discouraged activities that might damage relationships with the city, the organization did not penalize nonprofits—most notably Chicago Lawn's lead agency, the Southwest Organizing Project—that did engage in more political advocacy work.[30]

Still, its primarily anti-advocacy work may have helped situate the Local Initiatives Support Corporation as a community development intermediary among Chicago's power elite, particularly in city departments. As the organization's stance indicated, trust in these relationships flows upward, toward those with the most power (see Figure 2.4). Trust, therefore, is linked to privilege and power—in the case of Chicago and many other cities across the nation, this relationship implicitly privileges middle-class Whiteness and reinforces systems of control that perpetually marginalize communities of color and the poor. Only minimal trust flows in the opposite direction. The corporation built trust with the city in part by striving not to work against "friends" in power, and in return, as the organization demonstrated a commitment to minimal conflict, the city came to trust it as an intermediary to neighborhood organizations. The Local Initiatives Support Corporation then built relationships with lead agencies to cultivate trust for the New Communities Program, and in return lead agencies benefited from its relationships, programmatic funds, and technical expertise.

TRUST, MISTRUST, AND COLLECTIVE SKEPTICISM

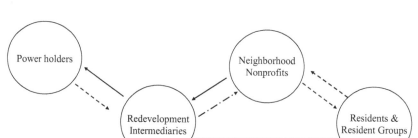

Power holders = city
officials, foundations,
and funders

⟶ High levels of Trust
⟶ Medium levels of Trust
⟶ Medium-low levels of Trust
⟶ Low levels of Trust

Figure 2.4. Diagram of power dynamics of trust in the Local Initiatives Support Corporation's network.

By restricting access to money, political clout, and technical expertise for controversial advocacy or policy work, the Local Initiatives Support Corporation and the lead agencies buffered themselves from challenging relationships and thus maintained their own power. Despite its unwillingness to challenge policies and systems underlying social, economic, and political inequities, the corporation expected trust in its method of community engagement and development—and, to a certain extent, it was able to maintain that trust because local nonprofits so badly needed the resources they could provide. Local nonprofits *did* gain access to those much-needed resources, but these groups, together with residents, were left to assume high levels of risk if their needs remain unaddressed. Relationships of trust thus implicitly privileged the culture and agenda of some network members over others and left those with less power to assume most of the risk.

This type of development may lead to relationships between powerful city departments and local nonprofits, but it cannot guarantee relationships that are equitable or development that is socially just. Indeed, it can even create the conditions—including a disenfranchised public— that the Local Initiatives Support Corporation and the New Communities Program theoretically aim to ameliorate.

"We Develop Our People": Benefits and Challenges for Lead Agencies

As the literatures on organizational networking and development suggest, local economic development relies on relationships for implementation and so can connect low-income areas to larger organizations with more political and economic power.[31] Through such relationships, development should thus open avenues of access to funds, technical expertise, well-researched development plans, and political and economic clout.[32] Connections to external networks have indeed proven to be fruitful for the lead agencies tied to the New Communities Program, yet whereas the Local Initiatives Support Corporation, the lead agencies, and city officials adopted a rhetoric of trust and norms of engagement, residents and other community groups saw limits to the program as a means for social change.

Enlace: Lead Agency in Little Village

The New Communities Program in Little Village encouraged a strong, politically connected organization to grow, refocus its energies on increasing human capital, and operate as a local intermediary for foundations, politicians, and grassroots organizations. That organization, known as Enlace, originally formed in 1990 as a community development corporation focused on housing and economic issues, and it had evolved to focus on secondary education and community violence. The organization had historically strong ties to Chicago politics and operated as a training ground for aspiring politicians.[33] When asked about the impact of Enlace and its ties to local politics, Little Village resident Diana Gomez excitedly said, "So, like there's this younger, twenties- to thirties-something generation that was raised with having like [Little Village native] Jesus Garcia in a State seat or as Alderman, or having Sonia Silva as the State Rep. And that really came from a lot of grassroots organization of like block club organizing and different community work. . . . This [history] really gives a shape to the identity of the community and affects the kinds of collaborative work that gets done." This history was shaped by, for instance, one of the people Gomez mentioned: Jesus "Chuy" Garcia, a former alderman of Little Village, the first Mexican American state senator, and a politician who would become a prominent mayoral candidate during the 2015 elections. Garcia's legacy includes his strong support of Harold Washington, the city's first Black mayor, and his progressive politics in the 1980s. As one of the founding members of Enlace and a lifelong Little Village resident, Garcia worked on issues surrounding youth violence, fair housing, and immigration.[34] Relationships to political actors like him helped solidify the organization as a powerhouse in the community and ensured its sustained connection to the city and the state.

In 2011, toward the end of the New Communities Program, Enlace employed 39 full-time and 110 part-time employees. The organization had an operating budget of roughly $4.4 million, with approximately $4.1 million directed to such projects as after-school programs, parent workshops, community-teacher pipelines, and coalition building.[35] According to its website, Enlace also worked on physical redevelopment, but several staff members I interviewed cited this work as minimal.

Enlace was able to engage successfully in relationship building because of its history in Little Village, its sustained community engagement, and its understanding of networks that included the city's growth elites. The organization could therefore implement the New Communities Program projects in ways beneficial not only to Enlace but also to the neighborhood and the Local Initiatives Support Corporation's network. Successful projects included the creation of small pocket parks throughout the neighborhood and its work on educational programming to support the Little Village High School.

Although the organization had already started to work on educational issues before the New Communities Program was introduced, the redevelopment initiative shifted resources and training firmly in that direction and toward the program's supported issues, away from affordable housing and physical development. Local Initiatives Support Corporation staff member Nereyda described, "A lot of the work [in Little Village] has been around sports leagues and sports development programs, safety-related work, all focused on human development. At least 80 percent has to be mostly just around programs that impact the people of a place—and less the physicality of the place." This ethos—prioritizing people over place—reflects the New Communities Program model. It brings what the corporation terms holistic and comprehensive human development into the community.

The movement toward social services and human development proved lucrative for Enlace. Employees were trained on ways to network across organizations and to create large-scale community outreach through the quality-of-life plans. Staff members were asked to lead projects and often received grants because of their relationship to the New Communities Program. While the program may have shifted the organization's focus in ways that weren't always supported by residents, it did streamline Enlace's mission and its ability to provide resources to the community. As longtime Little Village resident Hilary Muñoz explained, before the citywide redevelopment initiative, the organization had addressed a variety of concerns, some unrelated to a specific goal or mission. "I think that the [redevelopment initiative] helped direct the organization in terms of laying out steps, in terms of focus," she reflected. "[It allows] for a nonduplication of services and centralizes data."

In addition to training lead agency staff, the Local Initiatives Support Corporation encouraged collaborative programming. Its goals were to attract external funds to the neighborhoods and encourage community-based organizations to build upon their strengths. Rather than ten community-based organizations fighting over the same pot of money and each focusing on only one aspect of poverty (e.g., food kitchens or youth programming), the New Communities Program approach involved nonprofits pooling their resources to address neighborhood ills broadly and collectively. Enlace successfully embraced this approach and, in turn, worked to promote collaboration in the neighborhood. Enlace's alignment with the program provided new resources to the community; however, there were costs to its relationships with the Local Initiatives Support Corporation and the city.

Teamwork Englewood: Lead Agency in Greater Englewood

In an effort to include the neighborhood in the New Communities Program, Englewood community leaders from St. Bernard Hospital, Greater Englewood Parish United Methodist Church, and Pullman Bank (now U.S. Bank) approached the Local Initiatives Support Corporation and promised to support the creation of a new lead organization. With the bank as a financial sponsor and agreement from the corporation, in 2003 Teamwork Englewood was formed as the lead agency in this community. From its inception, the organization had strong ties to the three community anchors and to the corporation, but it lacked organizational leadership. Its board and executive directors lived outside the community and rarely spent time cultivating relationships with local residents.[36] The organization focused almost exclusively on education and social services, with after-school and summer youth programs, youth leadership training, and adult education. In 2011, Teamwork Englewood had a staff of eleven and an operating budget of roughly $600,000. Much of the budget came from the national intermediary, and funds began declining steadily in 2009.

Teamwork Englewood faltered within its first few years, but its relationship with the three community anchors and the New Communities Program ensured that the board had guidance and guaranteed the organization's survival. For instance, the Local Initiatives Support Corporation intervened in replacing several employees, as a senior staff member explained:

> So, we built upon Pullman National Bank [now U.S. Bank], had them be the incubator for starting Teamwork. They helped convene the core board members, many of whom are still there today, and they hired the first staffer, a woman by the name of [Angela Wells]. She's since passed away.
>
> She was a phenomenal, charismatic early leader that should always be remembered and recognized for doing an *amazing* job, for doing a very powerful planning process that led to their quality-of-life plan. That was very strong and very important. She was not as strong in the implementation, organization, management side. Things moved to a certain point but then stagnated.
>
> The next person that came on, [he] had some strengths in administration but a lot of other challenges. And then, unfortunately, they selected a former board member . . . who was quite frankly not capable for the job at all—and then they finally had him be let go with a little bit of support from LISC [the Local Initiatives Support Corporation].[37]

Xavia Charles, a young resident in her early twenties who had worked for both Teamwork Englewood and another lead agency in the New Communities Program, provided additional information into the organization:

There is a mismanagement of resources . . . how much money these organizations get on behalf of Englewood is amazing. Millions of dollars a
year pours into Englewood for services, community development—but
it's not trickling down to the rest of the neighborhood. I can say that
working at Teamwork Englewood, just the amount of money that I saw
coming into the neighborhood. Yeah, you know they might give out a
couple hundred here to a block club or, you know, do a half ass, excuse
my language, a half-assed program for youth and, you know, not want to
pay for anything. But yet they have this $10,000 grant that is supposed
to enable them to do this program.

Teamwork Englewood had a strong start, under the leadership of Angela
Wells and with support from several anchors in the community. After
her death, however, the lead agency struggled with organizational mismanagement and lost funding, which several community organizers and
residents mentioned to me during interviews and at local village meetings. This history, along with the Local Initiatives Support Corporation's
inability to find a preexisting local nonprofit that could manage the
New Communities Program, exacerbated organizational mistrust and
community frustration. The corporation's involvement in stabilizing
the lead agency demonstrated the need for surveillance and external
accountability, both to Teamwork Englewood and to other organizations in Englewood. However, this surveillance primarily remained
at the executive level, with Teamwork organizers—who were residents
of the neighborhood—attempting to implement sustainable programming without sufficient oversight or funding.

   Despite the intermediary's efforts to socialize organizations into a
common culture and build deep relationships in their target areas, the
development networks, both in local communities and with growth
elites, progressed unevenly across neighborhoods. In Englewood, some
community organizers became frustrated with the Local Initiatives Support Corporation's network management. Yves Davis, a program officer
in Englewood, elaborated,

   [The neighborhood network acts as more of] a selling point for [the corporation's] own fund-raising and proving its relevance to decision makers
   than it is of any real, direct value to its members. . . . [The network could

work if it were] designed to strengthen the organizations working in the neighborhoods—and, thus, the neighborhoods themselves. But it's not. The network is designed to strengthen LISC. Because, at the end of the day, LISC is just another nonprofit that hustles for grants.

This program officer saw the potential in the network that the Local Initiatives Support Corporation claimed to provide, but he highlighted several areas in need of improvement, particularly in Englewood. His account reveals a disconnect between the needs of community organizers at the lead agencies and the ways that the intermediary wanted the network, the socialization process, and the New Communities Program to work.

Toward the end of my interview with Betsy and Nereyda from the Local Initiatives Support Corporation, I inquired about this disconnect. Betsy's face became stern as she stated, "I'm a funder, but I'm also a nonprofit. I only have money based on what I raise; I'm accountable to my funders. At the end of the day, if I don't raise the money, I don't have the money to fund neighborhood initiatives either . . . The [New Communities Program] model is an example of trying to advance that work and the good things that can happen. It's still an imperfect universe; people still complain, but we've got things done." As this quote highlights, the New Communities Program provided a framework for community development that relies on external funding and a belief in a specific model. As a result, the program could be inflexible in its approach. This rigidity centered on the corporation's funding streams, desire to center itself as a local economic development expert, and belief that it was doing good work.

In Englewood, much of the community organizers' frustration was due to the lead agency's unwillingness to engage in grassroots community building and the Local Initiatives Support Corporation's unwillingness to advocate for the neighborhoods. As a result, Teamwork Englewood staff, Greater Englewood residents, and other community groups believed that the New Communities Program differed from other Greater Englewood agencies, and it was often at odds over the activities that Teamwork Englewood's employees would prefer. Yves continued, "There was a time when [the lead agency] was owned by the community. . . . [After Angela Wells left,] there was no stability in leadership. So people get tired of that and stop[ped] going to the organization. Yet we're still open. That means that [the organization] is not funded to do what [a local grassroots group] does; it would be nice if it was."

In addition to being frustrated with Teamwork Englewood's focus, residents were angered by what they perceived as a lack of community representation in development plans. As noted by a resident who is on one local nonprofit board and is an active member of another organization, "There's no community representation. . . . Community residents are not at the table when it comes to these development plans."[38] The executive director of another nonprofit emphasized accountability to the community: "People seem to be very unaware of what the development projects are in the pipeline, and they don't have a clue of what's happening. . . . Then you have these [city-led] plans. I don't see where there are consistent updates on where [the New Communities Program development plans are], so people don't know what's going on."[39] This frustration with a lack of updates and the perceived disconnect with the community led many residents to question Teamwork Englewood's presence and impact in Greater Englewood. In fact, resident frustration across both neighborhoods was often tied to perceptions of money and corruption.

Money for Collaboration

Organizational collaboration can work well when organizations come together organically to work on shared goals or issues. Given the current budgetary constraints of governmental and philanthropic funding sources, however, many grants require that community organizations demonstrate organizational collaboration. Typically, one organization is the lead on a grant and receives the funds, acts as manager, and generally disperses money to partner organizations. Yet as I learned from all the community organizers I interviewed, the New Communities Program covered administrative costs at only one organization. The need for funds meant that many organizations viewed collaboration as necessary for survival, regardless of whether or not a project aligned with organizational goals.

I met with Xavia in the summer of 2012; she had just come from a nonprofit board meeting and wanted to talk to me about coalition building. When I asked her for more details about how she understood collaboration, she leaned in closely and said,

> Collaboration is supposed to be about you entrusting another agency to do what you can't do, and [the other agency] trusting that you'll do what you can. I don't see that. . . . Instead of saying, "We can't do this," they [a local nonprofit] will find a way to finagle those funds so that they can be able to say they met that need. . . . Instead of focusing, they follow that next hot thing that will get them money. The organization I work for now is a prime example of that. Now it's education, last year it was technology, before that it was housing. And they don't do any of those things very well. But that's where the money is.

Similarly, Faith Brown, a community organizer in Greater Englewood, emphasized the imperative of funding as the basis for collaboration: "Coalition building in Englewood is driven by money. It's money. It's money! So there's some funding that comes in; the funders suggest that folks build a coalition to get the funding, and usually that's when people come to the table. I went to a meeting, and the first thing they wanted was my signature for a grant proposal."

Part of the benefit of the New Communities Program was that it streamlined funding to neighborhood organizations and created a strategic plan for development issues locally, which created opportunities for collaborative efforts to address certain social issues. At the same time, however, community organizations tied to the Local Initiatives Support Corporation were often listed as lead agencies on these grants. Therefore, as several members of nonprofits explained, grant funding for operating expenses funded only staff at those lead agencies, and programmatic funds were dispersed as the lead agency saw fit. Then, because these organizations were the identified leads, they often received both the recognition and the accolades for success. This funding structure, while attempting to address some of the issues raised by Xavia and Faith, worked to re-create the same issues that had already existed. And now that local nonprofits were expected to collaborate on issues, they would oftentimes jump at funded opportunities that they did not have the capacity to undertake.

Highlighting lead agencies as the go-to neighborhood nonprofits further embedded them in the New Communities Program network and in community development conversations at the city level. The designation also increased tensions between organizations. To receive grant money, members often felt compelled to work on projects that they did not support or on those outside their purview and expertise, and they often contributed significant time to a project. Without their organization listed as lead, however, they received less money and only minimal recognition, at best. In conversation with nonprofit staff in Pilsen, I learned that their organization had received no monetary or technical support from the lead agency or the Local Initiatives Support Corporation, even though they were fully responsible for aspects of a particular project. Nor had they received recognition for their labor. They continued to engage in the work because of their commitment to the neighborhood and its residents, many of whom volunteered at this nonprofit, but they received none of the benefit as an organization.

Part of what contributes to this problem is that lead agencies like Enlace and Teamwork Englewood appeared more trustworthy to city officials and grant makers because of their relationship with the Local Initiatives Support Corporation and the New Communities Program, which directed their support away from local nonprofits. As several people I interviewed noted, foundations often approached lead agencies with money to start or continue programming. Nancy Montoya, a prominent leader in Little Village, remarked that Enlace, for instance, often received public and private grants automatically or was made the lead on a project because of its connection to the intermediary and the program: "Because of Enlace's connection to the New Communities Program, money gets funneled to the organization. . . . It has to do with being at the table, those political connections, and being seen as an organization that can get the work done. . . . It's very difficult to separate relationships from [the] work because it's all part of the same thing. . . . The work that Enlace does and the relationships that [it] ha[s] make [it] privy to certain information and gets [it] at certain tables." According to both Nancy and an organizer in Little Village, relationship building made it possible for Enlace to do a better job with this power—it provided other local nonprofits with data, inclusion in projects, associated funding, and access to seed grants through the Local Initiatives Support Corporation. As organizations worked together toward New Communities Program goals, this process improved organizational impact and capacity and built relationships in the community.[40] Enlace also demonstrated to residents that it was providing the community with goods and services. These relationships indicated to potential allies that the lead agencies had deep connections to the communities they served. This perception, in turn, enabled lead agencies to cultivate strong relationships needed for community development. Enlace was thus able to negotiate its network position, increase resources for the neighborhood, and improve its standing as a neighborhood organization committed to social services.

For Teamwork Englewood, however, neighborhood accountability was far more difficult, as resident Virginia Adams commented, "Organizations like Teamwork has an idea of how Englewood should look or be developed. A lot of times organizations write Englewood into their grants, but they have not consulted with residents regarding what the true needs are of the neighborhood. In turn that leads to a lack of accountability. They're getting money because they wrote Englewood into the grant, yet because they don't have that accountability [to the neighborhood] there's no one saying, 'What did you do with this money?'" Similarly, I asked Xavia about her experience with funding for Teamwork Englewood:

> TERESA: Where do you think that money's going?
> XAVIA: [in a whisper] I don't know. . . . In the work that I'm doing now I work with an organization similar to the lead agency over in [another community] that is directly linked to [the corporation] as well. And seeing how they misuse funds, I can't say that embezzlement is happening, but I would say just in looking at how they budget the money, most of the money primarily goes to people's salaries instead of to what they received the funding, the grant for.

These suspicions were endemic in Englewood, but they also occurred in other neighborhoods in the New Communities Program. They showcased the larger problem of funding and accountability across all the Local Initiatives Support Corporation's partner lead agencies.

Conclusion

The Local Initiatives Support Corporation and the New Communities Program created opportunities for community-based organizations in target neighborhoods to connect with Chicago's powerful political and economic players. The program included residents in broad, citywide and regional initiatives; provided access to greater philanthropic funds, particularly from the corporation and the MacArthur Foundation; and created large-scale, comprehensive quality-of-life plans in two communities. In some cases, the corporation's role as intermediary improved conditions for distressed neighborhoods by providing local organizations with the opportunity to tap into the organization's network. Yet the New Communities Program also socialized lead agencies into the Local Initiatives Support Corporation model of relationship building, ensuring that this model expanded through both partner communities and the city as a whole, which did not always benefit the local communities and sometimes exacerbated preexisting inequities. These trusting relationships increased the lead agencies' popularity, particularly among city officials, who deemed them experts in their communities, but also redirected resources away from local community groups who were working before the program began.

Specifically, relationships between the New Communities Program and the lead agencies in Little Village and Englewood encouraged these organizations to (1) (re)focus their missions around social services; (2) network with funders, politicians, and developers; and (3) become the lead on other community-based projects. In Englewood, connection to the intermediary also shielded the lead agency from critique and failure. Here, relationships of trust were key to developing streamlined, comprehensive social service programming.

Within both neighborhoods, the connection to the Local Initiatives Support Corporation network and the ability to socialize lead agencies into the New Communities Program model allowed these organizations to increase staff, expand services, and focus on building interorganizational networks. Additionally, these relationships ensured that trust—in the redevelopment process and in the network—continuously flowed toward city elites.

These benefits and challenges weren't consistent between communities, however; the model operated differently in each. Those whose lead agencies adopted the ethos of the New Communities model and "trusted" their friends at the city level were rewarded, whereas those that either struggled with or questioned the New Communities model were left to flounder.

For example, Little Village's lead agency, Enlace, embraced the New Communities model of collaboration without contention. It focused heavily on approved programming and hired a full-time network coordinator to build relationships of trust throughout the community. During interviews and public meetings, I found members to be uncritical of the New Communities Program. Enlace thus maintained a strong relationship with the intermediary and became a partner organization for the program's next phase, the Testing the Model Campaign.[41] In 2012, Enlace received funding to expand its initial quality-of-life plan.

In contrast, despite focusing exclusively on programming friendly to the New Communities Program, Teamwork Englewood had a strained relationship with the Local Initiatives Support Corporation. Furthermore, it lacked trusting relationships with the city, residents, and other community organizations. In 2013, at the end of the initiative, Teamwork Englewood no longer had a dedicated network coordinator, nor did it receive many of the benefits accorded partners with the program. This did not, however, mean that the organization was completely shut off from inclusion in new redevelopment initiatives. For instance, Teamwork Englewood was one of the convening entities for the second Englewood quality-of-life plan that was completed in 2016. The differences in the viability of the lead agencies resulted partly from the distinct histories of the two neighborhoods and the two organizations—Enlace had already been an established nonprofit prior to the New Communities Program, whereas Teamwork Englewood had not. The challenges that Teamwork Englewood faced, however, also stemmed from staff frustration with the New Communities model and its heightened focus on social services as opposed to deep social change.

In both Englewood and Little Village, new local projects did ameliorate some immediate effects of poverty and crime, but neither the Local Initiatives Support Corporation nor the lead agencies addressed larger structural inequalities that produced low wages, led to housing evictions, polluted air and land, blocked access to public goods like transportation, and perpetuated racist and classist depictions of the poor.

Residents' and community organizers' frustration with the New Communities Program within neighborhoods like Little Village and Greater Englewood could have led to a total shutdown between community-based organizations, grassroots organizers, and the city. Yet, as I discuss in the next chapter, various kinds of organizations instead built upon their experiences in community organizing to develop tools of collective skepticism, central to which was a focus on local leadership development and increasing residents' skill sets as they related to urban planning. Collective skepticism and leadership development encouraged residents to challenge socially unjust urban policies. This approach was particularly useful given the Local Initiatives Support Corporation's unwillingness to jeopardize its own relationships with the city.

3

"You Can't Do It if You're Mad, You Can Do It if You're Organized"

Leadership Development and the New Communities Program

It was the classic idea of who outsiders perceive as stakeholders, but people who live in the community know who the real stakeholders are.
—Ernie Jones, 2014

During my time in Chicago, my flexible schedule and easy access to a car led community activists to invite me to meetings around the city. One of these meetings, at the University of Chicago, was coordinated by Isabel Nelson, a local attorney, activist, and founder of a community development corporation (CDC). Isabel's organization focused on environmental rights for Black communities both across the city and internationally. The session she led centered on helping residents benefit from a large-scale railroad expansion that was affecting predominantly Black neighborhoods on Chicago's Southeast Side. The session opened with wine, cheese, and networking, along with drumming and music by a Black folk band. Most attendees, residents from across the Southeast Side, ignored the opening reception and instead sat and waited for the formal meeting.

After about thirty minutes, the meeting commenced. Its uplifting theme was "coming home" to build a new community. Along with Isabel, speakers included area aldermen and representatives from the Environmental Protection Agency, the Illinois Department of Transportation, the City Colleges of Chicago, and the Respiratory Health Association of Metropolitan Chicago. The dark auditorium was packed with residents from neighborhoods in the New Communities Program: Woodlawn, Englewood, Washington Park, and the Quad Communities. Both for me and for the activists to whom I later described it, the meeting that was about to start was informative because it would highlight both the city's processes and its residents' frustration.

Although the session was initially a rather banal town hall meeting (albeit one with performances by local musicians and updates by various city officials), residents' anger bubbled to the surface and disrupted it partway through. Notable was one outspoken resident who had voiced his anger at earlier community meetings, charging local politicians with the city's ongoing neglect of poor Black residents. Refusing to sit quietly, he stood to challenge the speakers about the point of the meeting and in this way sparked others to express their own frustrations. The tone was combative. When Isabel attempted to redirect the audience's attention, she was met with, "Who declared you queen of the universe, just because you have university connections?!" More residents then assailed local politicians and even community organizations with their distrust of local government. One resident claimed to be hearing "the same old song and dance, where Black residents are again pushed aside." Most panelists were taken aback. Isabel, however, acknowledged the collective anger, and after a heated exchange with several residents, responded, "You can't do it if you're mad, you can do it if you're organized." Her statement seemed to quell the uprising, although murmurs of indignant frustration remained.

I left the meeting wondering how local community groups like Isabel's could organize in an environment of articulated—and understandable—anger and mistrust.[1] If someone like Isabel, who had focused her career on improving environmental conditions in Black communities, consistently had to assert her legitimacy, what chance did others have? I also felt torn: On the one hand, I sympathized with Isabel. Building a coalition, celebrating local culture, providing transparency through updates, collaborating across organizations, and speaking the language of power holders seem like effective ways of involving residents on development plans. On the other hand, Isabel's approach reflected a certain paternalism; this approach simply offered updates on decisions made without local input. Residents were told that they lacked expertise in development and were silenced, however ineffectively, when they expressed frustration. Although not explicitly connected to the New Communities Program, Isabel's approach was similar to the approaches of the program's lead agencies.

During my time in Chicago, I began to realize that the differences between organizations like Isabel's (together with the lead agencies) and those that were more successful in garnering the trust and involvement of area residents were related to leadership development. That is, it wasn't always clear whom the leaders of the community were or how to help them grown their leadership skills. As Isabel emphasized, hers was a local organization, and in some senses she could be seen as a community leader. Yet given the history of neglect and exploitation in Black and Latina/o/x Chicago—a point reiterated by both residents and urban studies researchers—community members had little reason to place their trust in either local government or, in the case of Isabel's organization, the nonprofit sector.[2] Who, then, *were* the community's potential leaders? How could local organizations develop them? And what, if any, was the connection between leadership development and community development?

Within urban (re)development, city hall often views neighborhood leadership as tied to key stakeholders—such as nonprofit executive directors, religious leaders, small business owners, and local elected officials—whose vision aligns with the mayor's office. This approach was evident in the New Communities Program, where local leaders were identified by external powerholders. As chapter 2 explained, the program's lead agencies relied on "development from above" and focused heavily on staff, social services, and relationship building with local nonprofits and with city agencies and officials. This approach to community development relies on vertical trust across organizations and attempts to attract resources through existing power structures. The same tactics, however, can easily privilege the plans and expertise of city officials, urban planners, and community developers. Thus, it places leadership in the hands of urban elites, not local residents.

In the neighborhoods of Greater Englewood and Little Village, the lead agencies and the grassroots organizations I encountered had distinct approaches to community development. The lead agencies were directed by internal bureaucracies that managed development plans and projects; in contrast, grassroots organizations engaged in "development from below" and were freer and more flexible. Activists from grassroots organizations combined community development practices with community organizing to expand local development initiatives and increase

Figure 3.1. Audience members at a community event in Greater Englewood. Photo by Roberto Medina, October 21, 2012.

resident leadership skills. Unlike the lead agencies, they encouraged horizontal trust between organizations and residents, at times flattening hierarchies, and they launched an array of actions conceived at the local level. Although organizing from below sometimes meant partnering with lead agency staff, when such partnerships seemed ineffective, grassroots organizers sometimes "went rogue" in ways that lead agencies deemed unruly, disrespectful, or even borderline illegal. Rather than rely on the leadership of external power holders, these grassroots groups developed local leaders who could influence development plans. The lead agencies' and grassroots organizations' different approaches to community development were linked to understandings of leadership (Figure 3.1).

Leadership, Organizing, and Community Development

The goal of local economic development is to improve the quality of life for residents in a specific geographic region. However, it does not necessarily challenge preexisting power relations.[3] Rather, organizations might seek to empower individuals to achieve their own economic advancement within an existing power structure and thereby establish such projects as GED classes, after-school programs, peace initiatives, and workforce training. Local economic development can also reinforce power relations among landowners, developers, local governments, and community groups, thereby actually restricting resident empowerment and impeding local leadership. Community *organizing*, in contrast, operates both to achieve economic gain and to challenge root causes of exploitation and oppression.[4] Central to community organizing is resident leadership development.

Local economic development and community organizing thus differ in focus, but they are not mutually exclusive. As scholars have noted, community developers can apply an organizing framework to their work. For example, a study of the Turning the Tide on Poverty project, which took place in the southern United States, highlights the impact of effective community-based local economic development on poor residents.[5] In this case, empowering rural residents to engage in decision making and to challenge existing power structures enhanced their political and social capital. A study of the regional equity movement similarly argues that equitable development is more likely when actors engage in deep "power analysis, leadership development, and community organizing" that ultimately influence social policy.[6] As these studies demonstrate, combining local economic development with community organizing can better ensure resident participation and positively influence unjust policies.

Challenging unjust power structures can be achieved by developing a community's capacities through leadership development and resident empowerment.[7] In the context of community organizing, effective leadership provides resources for skills building, works to build residents' self-confidence, and creates opportunities for activists' and residents' personal development.[8] By involving individuals in decision making and providing them with opportunities to develop new skills, leaders may also socialize members into new ways of interacting, negotiating, and strategizing.[9] Leadership is thus about cultivating relationships to acquire and maximize resources, such as skills, time, money, people, and political influence.[10]

Scholarship on leadership development urges a closer look at organizational relationships in low-income communities. Grassroots organizations, this literature suggests, can develop communities from the ground up and thus maintain some measure of resident ownership over decisions affecting neighborhoods.[11] Here leadership development aligns with collective skepticism; local neighborhood organizations use their skepticism of urban elites to engage and train residents in order to improve neighborhood conditions. These strategies might mean advocating for affordable housing, encouraging residents to run for political office, or working to change environmental policies or negative perceptions of a community. Within Chicago, grassroots organizers sought to empower residents and develop local leaders. Conversely, lead agencies attempted to restrict leadership to those affiliated with the New Communities Program.

Development from Above: Leadership within the New Communities Program

As chapter 2 described, the Local Initiatives Support Corporation engaged in a form of community development that involved neighborhood stakeholders, created social services for low-income residents, and highlighted development opportunities for local politicians. Within the context of the New Communities Program, this approach focused heavily on creating trust among participating communities and between these communities and city officials.[12] Given this focus on building relationships, the program's lead agencies created spaces where nonprofit staff, interested residents, small business owners, and other community stakeholders could meet and brainstorm ideas for improving their neighborhoods. According to local residents, politicians, and nonprofit staff, these meetings were particularly prevalent in Greater Englewood, after 2000, when grassroots mobilization around local issues began to increase.

Querida Villanueva, a senior executive at the Local Initiatives Support Corporation, discussed the New Communities Program in Englewood:

> It took a long time for Englewood to become [what] it is today, and you have to be patient and nurture the new local leadership and institutional infrastructure to get it going in the opposite trajectory. . . . In the last couple of years, there has been a total surge in local young leadership.

In Englewood, you're starting to see there's [a newly formed CDC and a resident-led grassroots organization], a couple of other groups that are being led by younger people, who, [because] their grandma grew up in Englewood, they decided to move to Englewood, whatever—they decided that they're going to do this neighborhood this time.

And that's to me the most exciting. I think Teamwork [Englewood] has helped to foster that . . . and so I'm a big Englewood booster.

As Querida highlights, new leadership efforts in Greater Englewood grew among young, energetic residents who hoped to transform local conditions. As will be discussed later in this chapter, this leadership emerged out of a deep frustration of historic urban neglect and exploitation by local powerholders. The Local Initiatives Support Corporation was able to claim this rise in leadership as linked to efforts by the New Communities Program. In the initial focus on comprehensive neighborhood quality-of-life plans, Teamwork Englewood brought interested residents together at their headquarters on Sixty-Third Street and Halsted to discuss multiple visions for their community.[13]

When I asked Querida about the impact of Teamwork Englewood in the neighborhood, she said, "[Teamwork Englewood] *created a space*; they have that great building; they have a place to meet. And *they just created a great hub of activity*, some of it functional, some of it dysfunctional, but it created a space and a plan and a set of things to try and do or react to" (emphasis added). The corporation and the lead agencies created a physical space where residents could review neighborhood concerns and redevelopment ideas with like-minded individuals. Many of these residents continued meeting separately from Teamwork Englewood to discuss ongoing concerns, particularly as they related to education, local development, and neighborhood violence. These facts were helpful in framing the narrative around the impact of the New Communities Program—they meant that Querida could claim that the new leadership in Greater Englewood evolved precisely because of the redevelopment initiative.

The New Communities Program provided its lead agencies with training and resources for social services, such as education, violence prevention, and workforce development (e.g., ESL training and computer literacy). Quality-of-life plans helped the lead agencies create blueprints for physical and human development, which city officials used to sponsor large-scale initiatives. Sharing of resources allowed the Local Initiatives Support Corporation to remain heavily connected to both local agencies and city officials and demonstrated clear wins for the program, such as large-scale resident involvement, increased social services, and collaborations with organizations and residents. Broadly shared resources thus highlighted the corporation's expertise in community redevelopment.

In these ways, the New Communities Program steered neighborhood initiatives from above. Doing so enabled them to provide the city with information on each neighborhood, including current land use, potential land use, and ideas for future large-scale development, and to present the city with a model for garnering resident feedback. Despite these benefits, however, they often ultimately ignored residents' views altogether.

Development from Below: Leadership and Grassroots Organizations

While the New Communities Program convened meetings for identifying residents' desires and drafted quality-of-life blueprints, grassroots organizations in Greater Englewood and Little Village engaged in strategies of collective skepticism to empower residents through leadership development. Outside the program, these organizations educated residents about citywide policies and politics by demonstrating strategies that applied the language of power holders, thereby illustrating the ways technocrats, politicians, and city officials communicate. Grassroots organizations also encouraged residents to get involved in representing their neighborhoods by positively presenting Black and Brown bodies in public spaces and framing their own development goals.

These efforts fostered a sense of community ownership. When asked to differentiate her approach to leadership development from that of the New Communities Program, Yazmin Cadiz, an environmental justice organizer, rolled her eyes and elaborated,

> The lead agency and the New Communities Program are the ones with perceived power, power being money. They have the money, but we know that money is just a stack of bills at the end of the day. And we know that

power is having a real leader, you know, who focuses on organizing and empowering people, not counting a billion dollars. . . .

I think that a leader [of a] community organization has more responsibility than making a lot of clubs. It's great that we have a lot of things for kids to do; we have murals and things of that nature. But we have more responsibility than that. Having activities doesn't change the conditions of our neighborhoods; it just gives people something to do.

Unlike the New Communities Program, grassroots organizations in both Greater Englewood and Little Village promoted leadership development first through educating and including residents in a variety of community actions and, subsequently, through transforming community development practices. Part of this work extended an organizing framework that aimed to eradicate social inequalities and value resident skill sets and views on neighborhood issues. Grassroots organizations also sought to show residents the importance of working with people and organizations outside the community in pursuit of certain goals.

This approach to organizing and leadership development was evident across Greater Englewood and Little Village. Grassroots groups engaged their collective skepticism of top-down models of community development in which residents remain uninvolved. As a result, although these organizations did work to develop relationships with local elites and with national and international organizations with similar missions, interorganizational ties allowed these organizations to maintain a high level of autonomy and still employ "development from below."[14] They could thus establish weak ties to funders and activate those relationships strategically rather than being taken over by them.

Such development from below aimed to empower residents and build local leadership. Grassroots organizations educated residents about politics, urban policy, and processes related to land use, and they worked with residents to address negative perceptions of their neighborhoods. These initiatives promoted leadership and collaboration, both across neighborhoods and among working-class and low-income residents. Unlike organizations affiliated with the New Communities Program, grassroot organizations built trust horizontally and so generated greater social capital for residents and area nonprofits. Highlighting their impact then also encouraged and supported resident decision making.

Resident involvement, through leadership development, and relationship building provided opportunities for grassroots organizations to
engage in complementary actions to the redevelopment initiatives. This
process operated to reduce power inequities, build resident skill sets,
and increase the city's accountability to low-income residents.

The Little Village Environmental Justice Organization (LVEJO)

In 2010, several grassroots organizations in Little Village aimed to influence local development projects by engaging in advocacy on a range
of social issues or working on land use planning. One such organization was the Little Village Environmental Justice Organization (LVEJO).
This outgrowth of the first National People of Color Environmental Leadership Summit, which had been held in Washington, D.C., in
1991, formed in 1994.[15] At the time of the New Communities Program,
under the leadership of Kimberly Wasserman, the organization sought
to combat environmental racism in Little Village by connecting local
concerns to global issues and by countering its root causes—poverty and
inequality—as a precondition for achieving greater social and economic
equity. LVEJO worked toward its goals using many tactics, including
door-to-door organizing. Although it has since grown, the organization at the time operated with a small budget (nearly $209,000 in 2011)
and employed a staff of six, who worked from the basement apartment
of a three-flat building in Little Village.[16] It was a small but effective
organization.

Members of LVEJO understood their work as a way to empower residents. As a result, staff members, many of whom were neighborhood
residents, were chosen for their potential to lead and their interest in the
community. Additionally, the organization was selective in identifying
projects, community members, and partner organizations. For instance,
the executive staff and board of directors would turn down opportunities that did not address structural barriers to local issues. Yazmin
Cadiz, Little Village resident and former LVEJO organizer, elaborated,
"[Rather than focusing on programs or specific projects—for example,
a local antiviolence initiative—LVEJO tries] to address, to focus on the
root cause of the issue rather than just violence itself. So, for example,
instead of putting up posters that say call the police, we want to know

why. What's the education like? How accessible are other educational institutions, or other communities?" As Yazmin hinted at, addressing the root cause of poverty through, for instance, the expansion of educational institutions can provide more long-term opportunities. Organizers for LVEJO looked critically at social issues and questioned the effects of the local environment on neighborhood residents. For them, activism was not about temporary or immediate solutions to community problems—such as putting up posters—but about first asking why these concerns existed and then seeking to remedy the resulting social problems.

LVEJO's Bus Initiative

To fulfill its commitment to environmental justice, LVEJO focused on public transit, air and ground pollution, and access to green spaces. This focus enabled the organization to work on projects consistent with its mission and address concerns also highlighted in the New Communities Program's quality-of-life plans. For instance, residents of Little Village, along with other community organizations, wanted to see improvements to the Thirty-First Street mixed-use corridor and more public transportation in the neighborhood. LVEJO was ideally situated to be part of such improvements, so drawing on initial conversations in the community, the organization partnered with other groups situated along Thirty-First Street to promote the reinstatement of a bus line.

To successfully influence the transit routes, LVEJO organizers worked with a variety of local actors. The public transit initiative was a five-year collaboration by community activists, local youth, college interns from nearby universities, and representatives from neighborhood organizations along the intended bus route.[17] The most notable organization was the Bridgeport Alliance, located in the Bridgeport neighborhood on the Southeast Side of the city.[18] A coalition-based organization, the Bridgeport Alliance included both Bridgeport residents and activist organizations such as Clean Power Chicago, CivicLab, the Chicago Teacher's Union, Southsiders Organized for Unity and Liberation (SOUL), Benton House, and First Lutheran Church of the Trinity.

Before the initiative, Chicago had no direct bus line to move people from the suburb of Cicero or the neighborhoods of North Lawndale and Little Village—all predominantly Mexican American and Black communities—to Lake Shore Drive, which borders beaches and large public parks, including the Museum Campus.[19] As a result, public transit commutes from these neighborhoods averaged one to two hours, depending on the time of day; such long commute times created barriers for residents who wanted to attend college or who held jobs in the central business district downtown, colloquially referred to as the Loop. Additionally, the local public high school—the Little Village Lawndale High School—was the only public school in the city without ready access to public transportation.

Lucia Alarcón helped me understand this context and the importance of coalition building for LVEJO's work. I had first met her at a transit-focused meeting in a local church in the Bridgeport neighborhood. A small-statured woman, she had commanded the room with clipboard and markers in hand. She used a moveable easel and magnified maps of the proposed bus route. Throughout the meeting, she invited attendees into the conversation and carefully laid out steps toward pressuring the Chicago Transit Authority (CTA) on the Thirty-First Street bus. After the meeting, I asked her about the coalition and the transit initiative; Lucia explained, "What works is my collaboration with people from various neighborhoods [including folks in the Bridgeport Alliance], college-age students, young students, and with Cambiando Vidas [Changing Lives], which is a Latino-based disability group. Through our collaborations and our work, we are able not just to demand but also have results."[20] In reaching across neighborhood and racial lines, LVEJO was able to successfully organize residents across a variety of affected communities. Linked to collective skepticism, this approach to collaboration centered on LVEJO's understanding that a broad network of residents and organizations provided a greater opportunity for success.

We met up two weeks later at LVEJO's headquarters to talk further about the transit initiative. Lucia had recently taken over the campaign from another community organizer. When I asked how her approach differed from those of her colleagues and how she proposed to move the initiative forward, Lucia animatedly explained,

> I hear people say [the CTA] are just a bunch of businessmen. They don't care about people. . . . I like to be more practical. . . . And I say, well, if they're a businessman, then you approach them with a business plan. You

know? . . . You want a business plan, I will give you a business plan, and then we're going to be talking the same language. . . . If he's a business-man, then he's going to understand business, and business-wise this is economically viable for the parties involved. . . .

I don't think [this strategy] is going to work in every campaign that people do. But it works for the transit campaign because transit is all about money. It's all about politics. But the underlying part of that—the part that I don't go out there and scream to these authorities [at CTA] about—is that it also builds unity, and it's also about uniting people of color, and it's about access. I'm not going to tell them about that; I'm going to tell them how much money they're going to make.

Recognizing that the CTA cared more about generating income than about uniting communities of color, Lucia engaged in strategic code-switching, using technical language to frame the initiative as a means for economic viability. Code-switching combined with collaborative efforts across the affected neighborhoods ensured that Lucia could suc-cessfully frame the project as a win for all parties. With limited funds, Lucia engaged the technical expertise of university interns—especially one particular Latina student from Cicero, who was studying urban planning—to create a business plan. It presented data supporting an out-line for potential ridership and specific bus routes, which was language the CTA could understand. As Lucia highlighted, taking a combative approach—particularly one focused on classism and racism, or on "the people"—could impede the initiative by slowing the process or closing channels of communication, which is precisely what happened before Lucia became public transit coordinator in 2012.

LVEJO's Tactics and Leadership Development

Unlike the New Communities Program lead agencies, LVEJO com-plemented its noncontroversial tactics with more visible, traditional advocacy (Figures 3.2, 3.3, and 3.4). Although Lucia knew that transit was all about money for the CTA, she also knew that the transit coali-tion needed to build and sustain resident momentum. To accomplish this goal, LVEJO sponsored a collective walk and bike ride and asked residents from the affected neighborhoods to joyously march along the

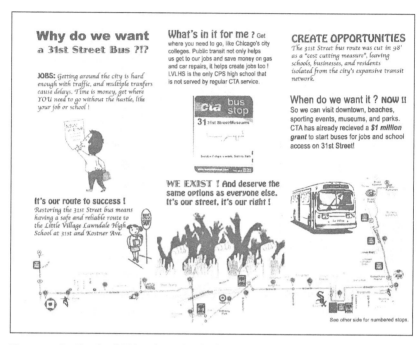

Figure 3.2. Inside of trifold brochure that highlights the benefits of the Thirty-First Street bus. Created by LVEJO during their public transit campaign.

intended route, thereby signifying their potential as bus riders. This event included music, dancing, and chanting. In preparation for the vote on reinstating the bus line, activists recorded a video of this action and sent it to the head of the CTA. As an organization rooted in a Mexican American community, LVEJO created culturally relevant signage and imagery. All text was in both English and Spanish and highlighted public transit as both a right and a pathway to success.

Members of the transit coalition and residents of Little Village then demanded the opportunity to speak during the CTA board meeting, where they described the difficulties posed by lack of public transit when they tried to access resources outside their neighborhoods.[21] Members from LVEJO and each of the organizations in the Bridgeport Alliance dressed in white, carried signs in support of the bus, and congregated in the lobby outside of the board meeting. The crowd included fifty residents from the affected neighborhoods. Within this crowd, Lucia maintained a sense of order and calm while she identified the individuals

Figure 3.3. Poster of proposed bus route with Aztec symbols surrounding a CTA sign. Created by LVEJO staff as part of their public transit campaign.

who would speak to the board. Rather than highlighting community activists, she tapped several teenagers and young adults, a disabled resident who uses a wheelchair, and several parents to speak about the importance of the bus for themselves and their communities. Encouraging residents to speak at the board meeting provided a twofold benefit: it empowered residents to speak up for their rights and demonstrated to the CTA board a tangible need that existed beyond community activism. At the end of the board meeting, CTA officials promised to consider reinstating the bus line.

¿Cuando Lo Queremos? ¡AHORA!

Llegue a donde necesita que ir, como su trabajo, colegio, museos, y playa. ¡Nuestra calle, nuestro derecho!

When do we want It? NOW!
Get where you need to go, like your job, college, museums, and the beach. Our street, our right!

Para mas información contacte a:
Organización de Justicia Ambiental de la Villita

[redacted]
Transit Campaign Organizer
2856 South Millard Avenue
Chicago, IL. 60623

Phone: [redacted]
Fax: [redacted]
publictransit@lvejo.org
www.lvejo.org
Little Village Environmental Justice Organization
For more information contact:

[redacted]
5807 W. 35th Street
Cicero, IL 60804

Phone: [redacted]

Fax: (708) 656-7608

Para exigir que nos regresen el autobús de la calle 31 contacte a:

[redacted]
567 West Lake Street
Chicago, IL 60661

Phone: [redacted]

[redacted]
567 West Lake Street
Chicago, IL 60661

Phone: [redacted]

To demand that the CTA give us the 31st bus route back please contact the CTA:

Llamele a su Congresista y Concejal para exigir que nos regresen el autobús de la calle 31.

Rep. Luis Gutierrez: [redacted]
Rep. Danny Lipinski: [redacted]
Rep. Davis Lipinski: [redacted]
Rep. Bobby Rush: [redacted]

Ald. Ricardo Munoz: [redacted]
Ald. George A. Cardenas: [redacted]
Ald. Robert. Fioretti: [redacted]
Ald. James Balcer: [redacted]
Ald. William Burns: [redacted]
Ald. Michael Chandler: [redacted]

Call your Congressman and Alderman to demand they reinstate the 31st Street Bus.

Figure 3.4. Back of poster of proposed bus route with contact information for local political representatives. Created by LVEJO staff as part of their public transit campaign.

The march and board meeting showed the depth and breadth of potential ridership, generating solidarity among riders from the affected neighborhoods. The campaign thus began to forge unity for a specific cause across disenfranchised groups. LVEJO's actions ultimately affected policy—in 2012 the city temporarily reinstated the bus line (number 35) and in October 2013 made the route permanent.

In addition to increasing public transit to the community, the bus initiative empowered local residents and increased community members' understanding of city processes. Using their collective skepticism of the CTA to expand public transit into their neighborhood, LVEJO strategically trained residents of Little Village in code-switching, research, design, and development decisions and offered opportunities to learn leadership skills. The organization could then capitalize on these skills while training residents in using the tactics of the campaign. This strategy engaged residents in all aspects of the initiative: the student intern from Cicero researched the route and its economic viability, residents participated in the walk and bike ride, and local parents and youth spoke to the CTA board about the difficulties posed by the lack of public transportation serving their communities.

The Resident Association of Greater Englewood (R.A.G.E.)

After the implementation of the New Communities Program in Englewood, the neighborhood saw a rise in grassroots activity. In 2010, to address issues around development and in response to resident frustration with existing community organizations, lifelong resident Asiaha Butler, along with several like-minded individuals, formed the Resident Association of Greater Englewood (R.A.G.E.).

Although R.A.G.E. is an acronym for the association, it's an intentional one. It connotes members' extreme frustration with the city's neglect of the neighborhood and an intense passion for their community. Members, who were overwhelmingly young (with most in their late twenties to mid-thirties) and Black, consistently played with language and definitions, and they often highlighted the alternative meanings of the word "rage," such as when it refers to a craze or an early-adopted fashion (as in "it was all the rage").[22] As indicated in a press release from December 27, 2010 (Figure 3.5), "Greater Englewood residents are sick and tired of being

Greater Englewood Residents has R.A.G.E.!

Chicago, Illinois (December 27, 2010)- Greater Englewood residents are sick and tired of being sick and tired and now they have rage! R.A.G.E (Residents of Association Greater Englewood) is a newly formed resident driven association established to build relationships with fellow residents, Englewood's public officials, business owners and organizations. Members of R.A.G.E meet monthly to discuss and strategize on how to improve the community. Additionally, they discuss ways to keep fellow residents informed about the latest news in Englewood.

A need for change in Chicago's Englewood community is apparent and a voice for the community is long overdue. R.A.G.E is the voice speaking out to empower, educate, uplift and motivate fellow residents and stake holders on many of the issues that face the community. Members of R.A.G.E. contribute many of these issues to the lack of collaboration of the six wards within the community. "How can any these aldermanic wards serve our community and we don't even have an office here", stated Antoine Butler.

Saturday, January 15, 2010, at Englewood United Methodist Church at 4pm R.A.G.E. will host part one of the "Who's Running?" Summit. This is an open forum for residents and the current runners for each of the wards that serve Englewood. The January 15th forum will focus on the candidates of the 3rd, 6th and 20th ward. Part two will be Thursday, January 27, 2010 for candidates running for alderman in the 15th and 16th ward. Saturday, February 12th will be the last forum for the candidates running for alderman in the 17th ward. The times and locations for part two and three will be announced at a later date.

The general election is February 22nd and everyone in the community is encouraged to participate and be a part of the candidate forum. Members of R.A.G.E. are determined to demonstrate their commitment in improving conditions and to assure residents understand the vision of these candidates who wish to represent Greater Englewood. Residents will have the opportunity to speak with the candidates and discuss their goals, platforms and other issues affecting the Englewood Community. "Residents should feel empowered again, R.A.G.E. goal is to make sure their voices will be heard at these summits", Corrinn Cobb affirmed.

"We pride ourselves in being a resident only association; driven to become a voice of change and reason. We want a "Greater" Englewood Community and will do what we need to do to see that happen!" Phillip Sipka pointed out. R.A.G.E. values the contribution of all residents and seeks additional support from other resident leaders who are ready to take action and join R.A.G.E. in their efforts.

For more information on R.A.G.E contact:

Asiaha Butler
Phone: [redacted]
Email: joinrage@gmail.com

####

Figure 3.5. R.A.G.E. press release, December 27, 2010.

sick and tired, and now they have rage!" The press release highlighted the association's commitment to political engagement and resident representation as well as its combative approach to neighborhood politics. Rather than using established approaches to community action, which were perceived to be ineffective, R.A.G.E. members used approaches that highlighted their youthfulness, anger, and innovative energy. They focused on responding to high levels of crime, poor educational opportunities, and lack of local businesses and jobs in the community.

At the time of the New Communities Program, R.A.G.E. was not a formal organization but rather a resident-driven project operating without a budget or office space. The organization included more than one hundred members, five unpaid prominent organizers, and two high school interns who were paid a stipend through membership dues (fifteen dollars for nonresidents and twenty for residents). Many of the organization's founding members were either current or former employees or volunteers with Teamwork Englewood, the neighborhood's lead agency in the New Communities Program.

The central, active members of R.A.G.E. had jobs in a variety of occupations across the city, and they donated their time to organizing.[23] Some were staff at area nonprofits, and they committed to R.A.G.E. because it was seeking to fill needs that other organizations could not. As a collective that depended almost entirely on volunteers, R.A.G.E. struggled to retain organizers to perform much of the day-to-day work, yet the organization still maintained an active presence in the community, countering negative perceptions of the neighborhood and educating residents about civic matters (Figure 3.6). Its events included summer programming at local parks and efforts to redevelop abandoned and vacant lots.

When asked about the formation of R.A.G.E., Xavia Charles, a cofounder and onetime employee of Teamwork Englewood, reflected,

We started in the winter of 2010. . . . It started out as a group of colleagues, I would say; we were already working in the community doing various [types of] volunteer work. [We were] meeting each other at places like [Teamwork Englewood], church, and just being involved. I knew Asiaha for a while at that point, and she included me in the loop of getting involved in a community organization that was more resident-focused

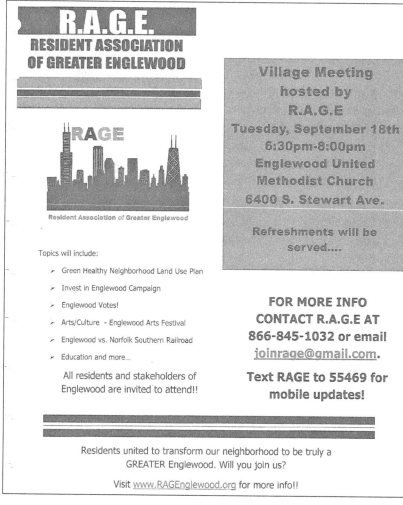

Figure 3.6. R.A.G.E. village meeting flyer, 2012.

because we felt like, with the vast amount of services and agencies in Englewood, a lot of them were not resident-focused.

So through that with this nonformal, or unformal, I should say, conversations, we ended up starting R.A.G.E. And how that got started, we were like what can we do to, you know, hold people with power, people with money, accountable?

Many members of R.A.G.E. had met through volunteer work with Teamwork Englewood and felt that, despite its stated commitment to community representation, the lead agency for the New Communities Program lacked such representation in day-to-day activities. In contrast, members of R.A.G.E. believed that its structure would allow the organization to remain a voice for the community without having its mission co-opted by funders. They appreciated this opportunity to engage in policy and political reform for Englewood.

Leadership and Political Engagement

As described earlier, Chicago is divided into fifty municipal legislative districts called wards, with one elected alderman representing each ward. With few exceptions, most neighborhoods correspond to a single ward.[24] Greater Englewood, however, is divided into six. Each aldermanic representative serves only a small portion of Greater Englewood, with most constituents residing in neighboring communities, and during the New Communities Program there was no aldermanic office in the community (as of 2020, this fact remains). This political fragmentation within the neighborhood has resulted in resident frustration with their local representatives.

Greater Englewood's history of political alienation and fragmentation, the lack of aldermanic accountability to the neighborhood, and the ease with which local aldermen claimed ignorance of citywide redevelopment prompted some residents and community organizations to get involved in local politics. R.A.G.E. members recognized that the community's lack of political representation had contributed to urban decay and pollution from the nearby freight yards. To address these unjust developments, R.A.G.E. members sought to promote better political representation by offering residents opportunities to hear from politicians and learn about the policies that affected their daily lives.

For example, in the lead-up to the 2011 local elections, the organization's first action was a three-part summit for aldermanic candidates to discuss their platforms. Held at two local churches and a community room at the local police station, the three summits attracted residents from throughout the community. Engaging their collective skepticism of local politicians, R.A.G.E. invited aldermanic candidates in all six of

Englewood's wards to share their platforms. Residents, in turn, could ask questions and challenge the candidates. Seeking to hold incumbents accountable for their lack of attention to community needs, residents raised concerns about criminal justice, public education, and corruption in the offices of various politicians. Many residents expressed anger over their inadequate representation, exacerbated by the revelation that many of the candidates for alderman lived outside Greater Englewood.

This action signaled Englewood residents' political engagement, countering the common assumptions that most were uninterested in voting and civic life. By creating a space for residents to become more politically involved, R.A.G.E. organizers demonstrated to elected and aspiring officials that residents cared about politics and the state of their neighborhood. The forums, therefore, not only increased residents' political awareness but also dispelled the narrative, popular among Chicago's elected officials, that poor Black residents paid little attention to political decisions affecting their communities. Where many residents had never heard from their aldermen, this mode of political engagement allowed them to confront politicians, lobby municipal offices, and achieve gains for the community. Its success then framed future projects and ensured that local aldermen would work with R.A.G.E. on community outreach.

Transforming Negative Perceptions of Poor Black Communities

As Englewood's quality-of-life plan outlined, residents wanted to both repurpose the neighborhood's public, often-abandoned spaces and transform its image as violent and crime ridden. In Chicago's popular imagination, Englewood was often touted as the epicenter of "Chiraq," equivalent to a war zone.[25] A slang term coined by Chicago-based rapper King Louie, Chiraq is used to describe the ongoing gun violence in Chicago as compared to the number of U.S. military deaths in Afghanistan and in Iraq.[26] Alongside this negative label, politicians, Chicago residents, and local news media further characterized Englewood as a community in need of social services and devoid of "assets."[27] For instance, when discussing my research outside the community, Chicago residents and police officers often expressed concern for my safety because "Englewood is just too dangerous."[28]

From R.A.G.E. members, I learned about efforts to counteract these negative perceptions by "actually building social capital" and "outlining access and exposing people to assets" and "changing the perception and being very deliberate in how we talk about the community," "highlight[ing] success stories . . . and positive stories."[29] Virginia Adams, a R.A.G.E. member and Greater Englewood resident, elaborated: "[We] just . . . really value individuals in the community and [do] not look at [the neighborhood] like it's a dumping ground for social services and poverty and homelessness. You know? Kind of lifting up the folks who are very . . . who are often looked over in Englewood—including everybody, youth, homeowners, workers, elders." For members of R.A.G.E., leadership development began with valuing residents' skills, knowledge, and presence. This valuation, in turn, included all residents—the homeless, young children, teenagers, the elderly, ex-gang members, the unemployed, and the underemployed—along with stakeholders in community development and local politics.

R.A.G.E. attempted to transform the perception of Greater Englewood by repurposing public venues (e.g., parks, streets, abandoned lots, community centers) as sites for community building. Activists ensured positive representations of residents through weekly community bike rides that included ten to twenty residents and through what is known as "positive loitering." Introduced by the Chicago Alternative Policing Strategy (CAPS) initiative, positive loitering includes residents idly occupying public space where there has been criminal activity.[30] This is a way for community members to combat drug use, gang presence, and other forms of misconduct. In Englewood, this practice is also about reclaiming abandoned, vacant land and reframing the presence of Black people in public space as cause for celebration rather than suspicion. For R.A.G.E. members, positive loitering thus has a twofold effect: it decreases crime and transforms negative assumptions and narratives of Black people leisurely enjoying outdoor areas.

Two R.A.G.E. members, Meredith Roe and Faith Brown, described this approach to taking over abandoned lots:

FAITH: We . . . play music, barbeque, give out food, give out literature to people, promote the association to others, and just make it a communal space in an area where people feel so-called unsafe.

MEREDITH: It's engaging the community and being sociable. . . . Deliberately trying to ignore or not feed into the stereotypes of what mainstream media says Englewood is. . . . Deliberately going to the vacant lots, purposely without really saying "Hey, we need permission." We do it anyway.

R.A.G.E.'s position as a resident association not formally bound to the Local Initiatives Support Corporation, city officials, or external funders allowed these activists the freedom to engage in such potentially controversial actions. They deliberately took over abandoned lots, without permission, to show that residents were capable of organizing their own events without external support. These types of takeovers also demonstrated residents' desire to claim ownership of their community. Due to their potential illegality, these events were typically less attractive to nonprofits that were well connected with funders and local officials. Because of their success, however, the Chicago Public Parks District approached R.A.G.E. in 2013 and asked the organization to partner in the Park District's "night out in the parks" events.

From this partnership, a formal initiative called "So Fresh Saturdays" emerged. During the summer, when crime rates tend to be high in the city, R.A.G.E. now hosts these free festivals at each of the five major parks in the neighborhood. According to members of the collective, the events are both about building community and about "reclaiming" open park space within the neighborhood. In a community plagued by violence, negative publicity in both the local and national news media, high unemployment and poverty rates, and an abundance of abandoned and vacant lots, R.A.G.E. deliberately created these venues that celebrate "what's good in Englewood."

Celebrating the good means promoting local African American talents (with a particular emphasis on Englewood-based artists), reimagining public space in new ways, and providing various forms of entertainment, with a focus on social justice. This promotion of local talent, reclaimed space, and Black people also served as a tool for R.A.G.E. to transform Englewood within the popular imaginary from a neighborhood plagued by violence to a more nuanced space of celebration. In their email and Facebook blast regarding one of the "So Fresh Saturday" events, R.A.G.E. purposefully shouted out, "Chi-Raq is dead. . . . So Fresh Saturdays in Englewood Lives on!!" For R.A.G.E. members, if people (including current residents, potential residents, visitors, city officials, real estate developers, and business owners) started to view Greater Englewood as a space of opportunity, growth, and "good things" rather than a war zone, then they would begin to invest both money and time in the community.

The monthly "So Fresh Saturday" events took place at local public parks and drew fifty to seventy-five residents, together with public officials, for a day of food, dancing, free books, art workshops, poetry recitation, and basketball tournaments. Although each event drew only a small percentage of Greater Englewood's population, the initiative increased community activities and promoted future collaborations. When residents approached R.A.G.E. to contribute to these events, R.A.G.E. members asked them to consider their own strengths rather than dictating how they should help. For instance, one resident mentioned that he loved outdoor cooking and would be happy to grill all day, so he became the "So Fresh Saturday" official grill master. Through these events, and in their attempt to rebrand the neighborhood, R.A.G.E. members and Greater Englewood residents engaged in civic action on their own terms.

R.A.G.E.'s publicly visible work—effectively rebranding Greater Englewood and challenging officials in public spaces—solidified the organization's position as a community leader. This position was made clear through multiple conversations I had. For example, I met real estate and marketing professional Zachary Evans for lunch at a downtown tea shop in the spring of 2012, to learn about the new CDC he had recently formed in Greater Englewood, together with his colleague and real estate lawyer Eric Jones. When I asked Zachary to identify a neighborhood leader, he thoughtfully responded, "We rely on our sister Asiaha a lot to answer questions. I would say we rely on R.A.G.E. to kind of give us some background on ongoing issues that have to be addressed in terms of economic development. R.A.G.E. is important because everyone in the association is a resident, for the most part. All of the people in R.A.G.E. are aware of the issues in Englewood. So a lot of this stuff that the CDC is trying to address, they've already done the groundwork for, like talk to people and gather information." Because it effectively included residents in all of its actions, R.A.G.E. had become a leader in Greater Englewood, without the aid of local politicians or support from the New Communities Program. Using collective skepticism of local politicians and city processes, organizers had created a political presence and redefined what political engagement meant in a low-income area. This process empowered residents to reimagine their community, question local politicians, and reclaim open space in their neighborhood.

"Poverty Pimping" versus "Keeping It Real": Two Models in Tension in the Context of the New Communities Program

The focus on resident leadership development by grassroots organizations in Greater Englewood and Little Village helped transform their local neighborhoods from below. Both of these neighborhoods have long histories of interorganizational mistrust, a point that residents and community organizers mentioned at local village meetings and events and that they emphasized during interviews. Exacerbating this mistrust was the requirement that the lead agencies in the New Communities Program incorporate its process into their organizational missions, as chapter 2 explained. With many residents also engaged in local non-profit and community groups, mistrust affected organizational relations, leading to a perceived pattern of "poverty pimping."

Poverty pimping is a slang term used to describe individuals or groups—often nonprofits or charities—that themselves benefit from acting as intermediaries between the poor and funders. To be a poverty pimp is to use poverty and the impoverished as tools to secure money from the state for social service programming aimed at the poor; it is thus a vehicle for economic advancement, available to those who can manipulate grant money to their advantage by directing funds to their organizations. Part of the problem with it is that it typically uses discourse and media campaigns that stereotypically depict the poor as violent and unruly, thereby advancing a narrative of community pathology in which poor people need saving from themselves. Missing from the agenda is an effort to address the root causes of poverty. In my conversations with residents and community activists, I heard furiously expressed critiques of organizations perceived as poverty pimps:

There's a Wild West mentality here. Or I dare say a poverty pimping sort of thing that happens, that people come in to save the natives. This sort of neoliberal way of looking at the world, very colonized. And so you have people that come in with the perspective of really helping these people who can't help themselves. There's a subcontext underneath all of this and affects the delivery of services and how people come to the table.[31]

There's a mistrust on behalf of residents because they're starting to see these same patterns. They seen [sic] that all these organizations come into the neighborhood and make these promises and say that they've gotten this money, but they [the residents] haven't seen any real change on the ground. So there's a lack of trust.[32]

There's no community representation; . . . community residents are not at the table when it comes to these development plans. Organizations [like the lead agency] has an idea of how [the neighborhood] should look or be developed. . . . They're getting money because they wrote [the neighborhood] into the grant, yet because they don't have that account-ability [to the neighborhood] there's no one saying what did you do with this money?[33]

Such statements highlight residents' anger and indicate their lack of support for the New Communities Program. On several occasions, I heard residents and community activists disparagingly talk about non-profits (including the lead agencies) that "went after that grant money" and used the "neighborhood as a line item" to funnel federal and phil-anthropic funds into their own coffers. A parallel critique charged the same organizations with using negative stereotypes of residents and the neighborhood to ensure their own continued funding. As one resident astutely noted, "If there aren't any problems, then there won't be any grant money to fund these programs." As we saw at the beginning of the chapter, this anger was directed at several types of community orga-nizations, not just those connected to the New Communities Program.

A self-interested model of nonprofit work, such as the one de-scribed by these residents, places the success of the organization above the needs and desires of constituents. As a result, programs that are developed in such a model are often temporary solutions to systemic, structural problems. Long-standing needs for jobs, living wages, public transportation, affordable housing, quality education, and a clean and healthy environment remain largely unaddressed.[34] Agencies engaged in poverty pimping contribute to residents' mistrust of nonprofits, philanthropy, and the state. Faith and Meredith, from R.A.G.E., expressed their frustration with the nonprofit field in their community:

> FAITH: A lot of things are driven by social servicing, so it's hard to get people to think outside of the box.
>
> MEREDITH: They [local nonprofits and governmental agencies] make us seem needy.
>
> FAITH: A lot of people are making money off of us and not really addressing our needs. There's nothing wrong with giving and philanthropy, but [residents] need to see that they're assets too and [we need to] think outside of these social services.

Residents' and activists' disparaging view of nonprofits that either realign their missions to support funders' requests or apply a deficit-based model to neighborhood development led to tensions between those perceived as "poverty pimps" and those that would instead "keep it real." These two phrases encapsulate the tension I heard expressed in both neighborhoods. Explaining this tension, a handful of community organizers reported that their organizations had consistently turned down grants that did not match their missions. This was the case for R.A.G.E. and LVEJO, and also other local nonprofits across Chicago. When I asked Willy Baez—community organizer, local educator, and executive director of a land use nonprofit—about the difference between the local New Communities Program lead agency and his organization in a gentrifying Latina/o/x neighborhood, he replied,

> Our mission statement and our agenda is transparent. We've declined funding from Coca-Cola and Boeing because their ethics are wrong, you know. Yet there's other organizations that will take money from whoever, and when you have those people that are running the development programs in the neighborhood whether it's economic development or just

like infrastructure development, at the end the funding they get is who they're working for. . . . The way I look at those organizations is the way I look at politicians. It's all self-interest. For us, we have declined several corporate grants because we want to keep it real.

"Keeping it real" in this sense allows an organization to be selective in the organizations it works with and the relationships it pursues. This selectivity allows it to avoid co-optation, particularly the realigning of its mission to reflect funders' desires. Additionally, it allows for the leadership development of local residents, as they are viewed as important collaborators within neighborhood processes. To "keep it real," organizations must center residents as the primary focus. At the same time, "keeping it real" sometimes strained relationships with local politicians and other organizations, both local and citywide. In some cases, potential partner agencies refused to collaborate with these groups because the agencies saw those groups as too radical, uncooperative, and unrealistic.

Diego Rojas, a young community organizer from a Little Village organization, reflected on the challenge for activists:

When you're dealing with different organizations, they're going to have their own agendas. It's just they have self-interest and have to keep their head above water . . . so when you're dealing with a project in the neighborhood, you have to make sure that everybody's on the same page, you know everyone's agenda. . . . Cuz there's always someone trying to pull some sneaky shit. Always. I mean it's unbelievable what they'll try to pull, some of these organizations. . . . [But] we work with all of the organizations; sometimes they have their own agendas, and so we're aware of that. *But if it's for the greater good of the community, we'll work with them.* (emphasis added)

Local community organizers like Diego pointed to the lack of resources, which constrained many organizations. Money was the biggest issue, but other resources were limited as well, including the staff and technical expertise needed to implement what many organizers viewed as "meaningful" change that could address deep systemic barriers to development. Largely because of these constraints, some nonprofit staff would "pull some sneaky shit," as Diego highlighted, to attract funds, prestige, and accolades, which could, in turn, lead to greater funding opportunities.

Such "sneakiness" included ignoring contributions of other groups in implementing collaborative programming, reallocating program funds to salaries for executive staff, creating "ghost programs" that existed only on paper, and spreading negative rumors about other organizations to drive away potential clients and partners. But again, the lack of resources—and potential access to some of what they needed—could compel some organizations to such measures in an effort to achieve their goals.

In thinking through ways to collaborate with different kinds of organizations and focus on local leadership development, agencies engaged in the New Communities Program often fell into one or the other approaches. However, both LVEJO and R.A.G.E. rejected narratives of "keeping it real"—which overly relies on local responses to local issues—and "poverty pimping"—which advances a narrative of race- and class-based pathology. Instead, as will be further explored in chapter 4, they focused on a more effective approach that included developing strategic networks of opportunity to ensure sustainable and viable opportunities for their respective communities.

Conclusion

Trusting in the Local Initiatives Support Corporation's model of redevelopment, the lead agencies in the New Communities Program employed a "development from above" approach that implicitly privileged urban elites over low-income Black and Latina/o/x residents. These agencies' efforts built vertical trust among foundations, urban elites, and select nonprofit organizations, and they also exacerbated local mistrust, leading to claims of poverty pimping, in development plans and processes.

Instead of closing channels for development, however, the Local Initiatives Support Corporation's top-down model created opportunities for grassroots organizations to identify gaps in neighborhood services and create spaces to engage in "development from below," incorporating residents and developing leadership. In both Little Village and Greater Englewood, local grassroots groups enhanced residents' skills and showcased the work of local community organizers whose initiatives strategically benefited their members, their organizations, and local residents.

In their campaigns, LVEJO and R.A.G.E. framed development projects by pairing visible social activism with less controversial tactics. In

Little Village, LVEJO campaigned for reinstatement of the Thirty-First Street bus. In Greater Englewood, R.A.G.E. sponsored positive loitering campaigns and aldermanic summits. Through these events, R.A.G.E. and LVEJO presented themselves as powerful, sustainable organizations, with capacities to effect change, and, using collective skepticism, they built relationships among residents, public officials, and neighborhood activists and nonprofits. These relationships provided opportunities to partner with external organizations and develop strategies complementary to those of the New Communities Program and its local lead agency. Using collective skepticism, trust in these relationships flowed cyclically, with each group intentionally engaging in reciprocity and reducing power inequities. Rather than remedying individual pathologies, these efforts aimed to enhance residents' leadership skills and built social capital and trust in local institutions.

In Greater Englewood, R.A.G.E.'s positive loitering campaigns may have done little to improve neighborhood infrastructure, but these actions promoted both asset building and the perception that marginalized residents are capable of addressing structural inequities. As with LVEJO's transit initiative in Little Village, R.A.G.E. began a conversation between residents and city officials. In focusing on leadership and skills development, grassroots organizations educated residents about citywide policies and politics, enabling them to shape the representation and development of their neighborhood. The work of R.A.G.E. and LVEJO thus fostered a sense of community ownership and created pathways for political accountability.[35] Particularly in places like Greater Englewood and Little Village, which suffered from social, political, and structural neglect, grassroots action highlighted the impact, commitment, and capacity of poor Black and Mexican American residents.

As I showcase in chapter 4, LVEJO and R.A.G.E. moved beyond the "poverty pimp" or "keeping it real" models of community development and organizing. Instead, they used collective skepticism to develop networks of opportunity. These networks allowed grassroots organizers to build collaborative relationships with groups that existed beyond their neighborhoods, gain access to new resources and ideas, and work toward common goals.

4

"Teamwork to Make the Dream Work"

Networks of Opportunity and Collective Skepticism as a Tactical Tool

Sometimes organizations don't want that resident input, because they know that when residents are engaged, residents can and often do take over that project and say what they really want to happen.
—Nikki Song, 2017

When I began conducting interviews, most of the people I spoke with preferred to meet at local establishments rather than in their offices. They explained that they felt more comfortable and at ease out of their offices and in public spaces. In Little Village, the popular destination was a newly renovated café. The owners had transformed what was once a dimly lit floral shop into a funky space with small round tables, interesting and colorful design elements, and delicious fusion fare. Over coffee and *jibarito* sandwiches, I talked with longtime community organizer Hilary Muñoz about coalition building and politics in Little Village.[1] When I asked about the New Communities Program, Hilary was silent for a few moments but then, whispering, raised issues of mistrust: "[Just because I don't fully trust someone or the organization that's] not to say that I won't work with them. But that I will be more cautious as to what I'll say and the depth of that relationship. And I'll think about that person a little bit more and think about how they approach their work and what decisions they make. I'll be more critical." Several other community organizers and residents articulated a similar sentiment: they opted to work together, and partnered with external organizations, even while maintaining their feelings of unease or mistrust. Although viewed as a barrier to community building and neighborhood progress, used as collective skepticism, this mistrust provides community organizations and residents with some protection against further urban neglect and neighborhood exploitation.

I heard the same view highlighted at many of the community meetings I attended. For instance, during a particularly animated gathering at a public park fieldhouse on the Southeast Side of Chicago, one resident stood up and exclaimed, "Our neighborhood's looked like this for a very long time, and nobody is working together to change any of this. Instead, things are worse. The city has closed schools, we aren't supporting the local Black businesses here, and people are afraid of going outside. It's in everyone's best interest [for residents, community groups, nonprofits, local politicians, and philanthropy] to team work to make the dream work."[2] Residents and community activists believed that successfully combatting the growing problems in their communities—from high rates of crime to low rates of employment and education—meant relying on a variety of organizational and political actors. Instituting systemic change, they believed, would require collaboration. However, they knew that such collaboration did not necessitate wholehearted trust in citywide institutions, and that was important because such trust was not going to be granted. Residents fully understood that elite actors' visions for poor neighborhoods often conflicted with local desires. Additionally, given long histories of neglect, many Chicagoans within low-income neighborhoods, especially in Black and Latina/o/x areas, deeply mistrusted the nonprofit and governmental sectors. Given that this mistrust was bound to continue, how could collaboration work? And how could activists like Hilary use that mistrust as a tool to help realize local dreams?

They could do so by maintaining collective skepticism, in which they held onto their mistrust of organizations that were focusing on something other than the community's best interests but still found ways to work with them. In this case, grassroots groups in Greater Englewood and Little Village used their networks to solicit varied responses to large-scale redevelopment. A critical component of their strategies in engaging with these tasks was their reliance on networks of opportunity and on maintaining their collective skepticism.

"Creating Our Own Sense of Movement": Using Collective Skepticism to Build Coalitions

Some community groups in Greater Englewood and Little Village leveraged their collective skepticism as they strategically built coalitions between residents, public officials, community activists, and development experts. These relationships, which involved powerful experts, ensured that residents were included in development decisions and provided added protection for equitable development to occur.

The trust built between residents and community groups with similar levels of power increases what criminologists refer to as collective efficacy—in other words, residents and local organizations work together to create informal social control mechanisms.[3] Collective efficacy may be important for building a sense of community (in which residents feel connected to and respect each other) and for setting shared expectations among residents and local groups with similar economic and political power. Neighborhoods with high levels of such collective efficacy have been shown to experience lower rates of criminal activity and greater civic involvement.[4]

Building trust between organizations with disparate economic and political power, however, operates differently. For instance, to direct much-needed resources to their organizations and/or neighborhoods, community nonprofits that network with powerful urban elites risk dependency and socialization into a framework that may be detrimental to local issues. As discussed previously, these relationships can lead to a change in a nonprofit's mission, away from conflict-oriented and resident-centered organizing and toward city- or philanthropy-approved projects. This process minimizes local dissent related to unequitable redevelopment decisions. Here, collective skepticism, rather than collective efficacy, works to build bridges while also recognizing the limitations of such relationships.

This alternative to poverty pimping and keeping it real aligns with the principles of àse, as discussed in chapter 1 and first introduced to me by longtime community activist Ernie Jones. Recall that, within Chicago, this Yoruba concept reminds residents of racially marginalized and low-income neighborhoods, of their personal power, or agency, and their ability to create meaningful change. Therefore, *àse* encourages residents and community organizers to strategically navigate relationships of power with the city to ensure equitable redevelopment. As a member of one grassroots organization told me, "We may not like [the lead agency], and we may be critical of the LISC [Local Initiatives Support Corporation] funds; however, we need to put that aside to ensure that the neighborhood receives the best programming and development that it can." In other words, even with their concerns regarding organizational missions or agendas, many organizers in these two Chicago communities continued to work with those they did not necessarily trust because they saw the collaboration as being good for the community.

For instance, when asked about the New Communities Program, Ernie reflected on trust: "There's those who don't trust, [but] at some point people say, 'I'm just going to see if this thing works.' So there's been a shift [in the way organizations work together] and in [the way organizations] look at how LISC [the Local Initiatives Support Corporation] can work for them." He also highlighted an active strategy on the part of residents and organizations: "[People] in [Greater] Englewood and Little Village are saying, 'Who says that they [the lead agencies] have to be the one? Who's anointed them the place to be?' So that's sort of bothersome for people, and some of these emergent groups coming out are questioning that [and saying], 'We can go to other spaces; *we can create our own sense of movement; we can have our meetings and invite them* [the lead agencies].' I think that's a good thing" (emphasis added). Instead of a breakdown in organizational collaboration, Ernie explained, groups could approach the Local Initiatives Support Corporation and the New Communities Program with an eye toward "see[ing] if this thing works," at least well enough for the collaboration to provide resources and achieve collective goals. Nonetheless, as skeptical organizers knew, lead agencies might not represent the community's best interests, so these organizers created their own spaces and identified their own goals and groups to support their missions. Rather than (1) pursuing trust in a context where it was unlikely to develop (or where developing it would interfere with their ability to advocate for themselves or could compromise their own mission) or

(2) perpetuating divisions between "poverty pimping" that focuses on community pathology and "keeping it real" that focuses on local talents, these relationships forged *networks of opportunity*.

Networks of opportunity are webs of purposeful relationships that focus on specific opportunities or common goals to promote an organization's mission. These relationships provide members of the network with access to new or novel information and resources. And because they are both goal-driven and rooted in opportunities, such sets of relationships can encourage collaboration between different types of organizations. Within the New Communities Program neighborhoods, for example, network connections allowed less connected and less politically and economically powerful community organizations to use their collective skepticism to build coalitions that could mitigate power differentials between themselves and the lead agencies—which had access to the resources and decision-making power they needed—and to leverage those connections to work toward common neighborhood development goals. Despite a history of urban neglect, these groups did not disengage from neighborhood decisions but firmly believed in their ability to influence development decisions. Yet they also understood that they lacked the political power and resources to successfully take on city hall. Their collective skepticism, together with a lack of resources, led these groups to search actively for collaborative, supportive relationships across a range of public and private institutions.

In Greater Englewood and Little Village, grassroots organizations used networks of opportunity to engage both residents and nonprofits in pressuring city officials to improve their neighborhoods' quality of life. In Greater Englewood, some groups partnered with city agencies, whereas others confronted city hall using local networks. In Little Village, groups engaged in a broad-based network that included city hall, national organizations, and local groups. Community organizations leveraged needed resources by using a variety of approaches to networking, even though doing so could be difficult and time-consuming. Additionally, networks of opportunity were strategically deployed to connect their local causes to powerful organizations across regional and national boundaries, thereby achieving the goals of those networks in ways that were true to their missions.

Networks of Opportunity and Organizing Strategies

The literature on local economic development highlights not only these kinds of benefits but also some risks associated with building interorganizational networks that link nonprofits and elites promoting growth in poor areas.[5] As we saw in previous chapters, connections to citywide offices, national organizations, and private industry do provide residents and community organizations access to a variety of resources (e.g., clout, money, information, technical expertise). At the same time, however, these ties can present a series of challenges—especially when not accompanied by collective skepticism, they can lead to loss of mission, agendas framed to accommodate funding streams rather than community needs, homogenization of community development plans, and loss of resident voices in planning decisions. In Chicago (as in many urban areas), such challenges are reflected in several large-scale developments, such as rail line improvements and creation of public parks, which are driven by political decisions and generally are not influenced by community-based nonprofits.

How, then, can local groups have an impact on these decisions, as described in the previous section? What strategies help to temper the power imbalance between residents and elites? In Greater Englewood and Little Village, grassroots groups were able to circumvent some of those pitfalls by engaging residents in response to local issues, such as negative perceptions of the community and lack of public services. And although the city constrained the Local Initiatives Support Corporation and the lead agencies in the New Communities Program from engaging in resident-led initiatives that were not in line with its broader development goals, grassroots groups built upon the New Communities methods to engage citizens in redevelopment issues and to challenge projects that did not fully represent residents' desires.

Those desires were reflected in the comprehensive neighborhood quality-of-life plans that residents generated as part of the New Communities Program process, as discussed in chapter 2. In both Englewood and Little Village, these detailed plans called for physical development projects, notably a new park in Little Village and an urban agriculture district and small business incubator in Englewood. Residents also sought access to employment opportunities that provided living wages, opportunities for career advancement, and investment in local residents (e.g., quality workforce development, better education, and access to healthy environments). The Local Initiatives Support Corporation supported the creation of these quality-of-life plans, but support for specific projects—especially the physical redevelopment initiatives—was limited. Only when these local plans aligned with the city's broader goals would the intermediary provide additional support for them.

Several citywide initiatives, including Green Healthy Neighborhoods and the Chicago Region Environmental and Transportation Efficiency Program (CREATE), and large-scale neighborhood projects, including a new park, aligned with the city's goals (and thus with the New Communities Program) and had a direct impact on Greater Englewood and Little Village residents. These projects had incorporated public planning during their initial phases, which seemed promising in terms of aligning with local goals, but this involvement was often framed—and thus constrained—by the convening public entity, usually the Illinois Department of Transportation or the Chicago Metropolitan Agency for Planning. This was most evident in Greater Englewood. Thus, while resident input might have been used during the planning phases, such suggestions were able to be safely ignored during the building phases. To compound the problem, aldermen in Chicago have little political incentive to ensure that residents' suggestions are implemented in such projects. Grassroots groups and community residents thus became tasked with advocating for their own agendas, and initiatives where such advocacy was successful had to flow through strategic partnerships that aimed to either collaborate with or confront public agencies. The following sections explore three such partnerships and their different approaches to collaboration.

The New Communities Program and Expanded Redevelopment within Greater Englewood

Chicago undertook a variety of citywide and regionwide initiatives stemming from the New Communities Program and the neighborhood quality-of-life plans. As each plan was created, the Local Initiatives Support Corporation officials met with the city's commissioner of planning to ensure that the city and the program were in agreement about how to proceed. These plans demonstrated to residents and city officials that the corporation and the lead agencies were committed to community representation, had the tools to include residents, and were interested in maintaining friendly relationships with city officials. Yet any residents under the impression that planning meetings would result in resident-led redevelopment were surprised to learn that their plans were merely recommendations. Residents were further alarmed to learn that the city used data from the quality-of-life plans to inform large-scale projects that were not necessarily aligned with their broader development goals. Instead, the corporation's focus on maintaining friendly relationships with the city—not with residents—informed the work it encouraged lead agencies to undertake.

Such city-sponsored projects included the ongoing Green Healthy Neighborhoods initiative and CREATE. Both projects were linked to the region's large-scale land use plan: GO TO 2040, an initiative developed by the Chicago Metropolitan Agency for Planning (CMAP). Formed in 2007 through the State of Illinois Regional Planning Act (Public Act 095-0677) and federally designated a metropolitan planning organization, CMAP aimed to "conduct comprehensive regional planning, to program transportation funding, to provide technical assistance for communities, and to provide data resources for stakeholder organizations and residents" across Northeastern Illinois.[6]

As part of CMAP, GO TO 2040 (which was completed in 2012) used inclusive, asset-based language that sought to motivate action toward a "high quality of life." The report provided a blueprint to local politicians regarding the types of development that should occur in their respective areas and that showcased a collective understanding of the good these projects could bring to the region. The citywide projects that emerged from this report and the neighborhood quality-of-life plans were aimed at expanding the city's economy through added park space, rail and green economies, and redevelopment of low-income neighborhoods. The plans relied on resident involvement and used language specifically to draw support from a broader populace; unfortunately, however, these projects continued a legacy of expert-driven development that further disenfranchised poor communities.

This process played out in the design and implementation of the Green Healthy Neighborhoods and CREATE land use initiatives along the city's southeast corridor. Resident experiences with these two projects were informed by personal exchanges and response rates. Although some residents felt supported and well informed, others were cautious about the impact that these two major initiatives would have on their communities and their homes. In response, and to ensure resident ownership of any potential added gains, grassroots groups had to take very different approaches to partnership.

Green Healthy Neighborhoods Initiative

In response to an increase in vacant land in Chicago's southeast corridor, CMAP, the New Communities Program, and the city (implemented under Mayor Richard M. Daley and extended under Mayor Rahm Emanuel) created a large-scale land use plan to combat vacancy and population loss. Implemented in 2010 as a neighborhood stabilization program, this plan was known as the Green Healthy Neighborhoods initiative.[7] Chicago's Department of Housing and Economic Development, together with the Local Initiatives Support Corporation, led the project, and CMAP provided technical support for it through its local technical assistance program (which had formed in 2010, with funding from the U.S. Department of Housing and Urban Development [HUD], to work with local government and nonprofits to implement the city's GO TO 2040 plan). With a $4.2 million grant from HUD, through its Sustainable Communities Initiative, Green Healthy Neighborhoods drew heavily on the quality-of-life plans in each neighborhood and focused public and private investments in three New Communities Program neighborhoods: Englewood, Woodlawn, and Washington Park.[8] The project aimed to develop 11.24 square miles, including 6.24 square miles in Greater Englewood.[9] Much of this land was owned by the city.

Building upon the work started in the New Communities Program, Green Healthy Neighborhoods project organizers relied on local lead agencies for community outreach and involvement. During the planning process (2010–14), members of CMAP, the Local Initiatives Support Corporation, and the local lead agencies held quarterly public meetings across the three affected neighborhoods, providing community members with updates and the opportunity to highlight local assets and areas for improvement. During these meetings, residents and members of community organizations would brainstorm ways to develop vacant land. These meetings led CMAP to create a comprehensive land use plan for the Green Healthy Neighborhoods area, suggesting new park space, improved retail zoning, improvements to local housing, increased resident land ownership, creation of an urban agriculture district, expansions to local manufacturing districts, and green infrastructure, particularly for storm water run-off. The Chicago Plan Commission approved the Green Healthy Neighborhoods project as a ten- to twenty-year planning strategy in March 2014.

Included in the planning report was support for a local food economy that encompassed production, processing, warehousing, and distribution. The Green Healthy Neighborhoods initiative planned to create an urban agricultural corridor along Fifty-Eighth Street by building, with mayoral support, on the success of the preexisting Growing Home Wood Street Farm. Then as now, the Wood Street Farm provided two major resources to the community: organic, accessible, affordable fresh produce and workforce development programming in urban agriculture.[10] As part of its community outreach efforts, the farm created a job training program focused on residents who either had a criminal background or were otherwise deemed "unemployable." Its students learned agricultural, money management, resume writing, and goal management skills. Wood Street Farm also worked with a legal team to help trainees expunge their records. Students were paid for their labor and received additional assistance with job acquisition. In addition to offering these resources, although Wood Street Farm was not a community garden, it provided residents and workers with access to a clean, green space within a section of the neighborhood that is otherwise devoid of such spaces.

Given the Wood Street Farm's success as an active urban farm, Mayor Rahm Emanuel augmented the Green Healthy Neighborhoods plan with a strategic "green" land use vision for Englewood. The *Chicago Sun-Times* quoted the mayor as saying, "In Englewood, you have Kennedy-King. It's becoming the center for hospitality and culinary. But, there's a lot of open land. So, we're gonna be investing a lot in urban agriculture that . . . takes advantage of Kennedy-King's strength."[11] This plan aimed to convert three more areas into urban agriculture sites and use money from tax increment financing to attract commercial development to the Sixty-Third and Halsted business corridor.[12] This public financing scheme reallocates local taxes to subsidize redevelopment, infrastructure improvements, and other community-improvement projects within low-income communities.

Transforming blighted areas in Greater Englewood and other Southeast Side communities into farmland would provide much-needed development, but such development would be insufficient on its own. The programs already in place at Wood Street Farm, for example, did more than just that—they provided agricultural training to local residents, ex-convicts, and others who had difficulty finding employment. Xenia Czelusniak, the community outreach coordinator at Wood Street Farm, highlighted the importance of jobs and economic power for local residents:

> We're really focusing on Englewood and this immediate area as, like, a place where we can have the most impact. In, you know, a concentrated area, rather than spreading out. . . . Our *main* goal is to train more people and produce more food. The big question is can we train more people and get them in a job elsewhere. But we'd also like to have a space where we could also employ people in a more full-time manner. About 30 percent to 50 percent of our participants come from Greater Englewood. *Healthy food is a priority, but, like, people also need the economic power to buy healthy food.* And that means jobs either here or somewhere else in Chicago. (emphasis added)

If the proposed agricultural district could engage the strategies implemented by the Wood Street Farm, residents would have greater access to locally grown and affordable food, agricultural training, and jobs providing a living wage.

Making such a vision a reality would have required mandates to ensure that locally owned businesses would be supported or given priority over large national retailers and that courted businesses would be required to implement pollution controls, hire local residents, or provide workforce development or employment to community members. But such mandates did not exist; city representatives and local aldermen did not believe they should. They claimed there was a higher possibility of employment at large-scale corporations, despite research showing that many such businesses import workers or claim that local skill sets and job requirements are incompatible.[13]

City leadership also overlooked other research showing that small businesses hire local residents at higher rates, support other local small businesses, and maintain deeper connections to the neighborhood than do large-scale corporations.[14] Furthermore, as the vast research on immigrant and ethnic business districts indicates, locally owned and supported businesses can operate as venues for building social capital among the poor through networking and access to information and employment.[15] With long histories of broken promises and sustained neglect by area politicians, situations like these—where lip service was given to local needs but nothing was put in place to ensure that local residents benefited from the investment—exacerbated mistrust in local government. At public meetings throughout Greater Englewood and Little Village, Black and Latina/o/x residents described hearing the same, familiar rhetoric regarding progress and growth, with few benefits accruing to themselves or their communities.

In the summer of 2016, I met with Jordan Ng, from the city's Department of Planning and Development, to talk about Green Healthy Neighborhoods and resident frustration with it as another urban renewal plan that could further disenfranchise Black and Latina/o/x residents. He acknowledged challenges on the Southeast Side of Chicago, particularly in Greater Englewood, around issues of safety, disinvestment, and lack of population density. At the same time, he was enthusiastic about what Green Healthy Neighborhoods could mean for the area. Given the availability of vacant and abandoned land in Greater Englewood, Jordan highlighted the opportunity to develop the neighborhood as an urban agricultural incubator:

> JORDAN: As an opportunity, there isn't anything like this in the city for creating an agricultural district and bringing farmers together. What we do here is special because it's a place where they could all work together, get support, and create a network of people. We're pumping a lot of resources into these opportunities.
>
> TERESA: Is there also support from the city for people from Englewood who are also interested in urban farming?

JORDAN: We're always advocating for people from Englewood, but there hasn't been a strong stream of people from the neighborhood interested in this. The point is we think there's plenty of opportunity for everybody.

Jordan highlighted *plenty of opportunity for everybody*. Yet when I asked if there was a specific plan to ensure that existing residents would benefit from new developments, would have access to workforce development in food systems, or would be prioritized in new hiring initiatives, Jordan shook his head no and said the city's hands were tied. There were few mechanisms to ensure that those who actively lived in the three affected neighborhoods would benefit from the redevelopment projects. For this initiative, then, "everybody" actually included only those who already had the means and training to successfully access any new opportunities. As a result, residents viewed the city's "advocacy of people from Englewood" as empty promises.

Additionally, although the city supported development in line with national trends, land was available for urban farming in Greater Englewood precisely *because* city hall and local politicians had neglected this part of the city for decades.[16] The city still had little political or economic incentive to implement community benefits for low-income residents of color. Thus, before the agricultural district was created, the communities had good reason to focus on generating a commitment to these community benefits. To do so, community members used their collective skepticism to organize themselves and network with local experts to pressure city officials into ensuring residents' access to new opportunities. For example, as will be discussed in the following section, R.A.G.E. members strategically *partnered with* city agencies to ensure that residents accrued some of the benefits brought into the community through the Green Healthy Neighborhoods initiative.

Partnering with Local Experts: R.A.G.E. and the Large Lot Program

As chapter 3 explained, the Resident Association of Greater Englewood (R.A.G.E.) engaged residents in a process of education, collaboration, and coalition building to hold politicians accountable to the community.

Using their collective skepticism of the New Communities Program and the Green Healthy Neighborhoods initiative, members of R.A.G.E. demanded inclusion on redevelopment initiatives in Greater Englewood. They attended training sessions on local zoning, spoke with urban planners about decision making, and partnered with graduate students in urban design. These efforts were driven mostly by a desire to increase resident leadership skills and ownership of the neighborhood, as community organizer Faith Brown explained when asked about improving conditions in Greater Englewood: "Really we're not going to be able to be top-decision makers if we don't own some of this land," she said after a moment's silence, "and so that's why other people are able to make decisions."

To increase local knowledge regarding public policies, R.A.G.E. hosted several training sessions on policy and land use for residents. These took place across various venues in the community, such as at Mt. Nebo Church Baptist and in the community meeting room of the Kelly Branch Public Library. Attendance ranged from twenty to sixty residents. Meetings included sessions with local groups such as CivicLab, a citywide research-driven nonprofit that works to build civic engagement, improve civic literacy, and increase government accountability. Trainings also involved CMAP on zoning laws, Neighborhood Housing Services (NHS) on foreclosure prevention, and the Chicago Department of Housing and Economic Development on ways that residents could work with the city on community redevelopment.

Using information learned during the workshops, R.A.G.E. members highlighted a twofold campaign, both to address the problems of vacant land and to increase resident ownership of the neighborhood. Greater Englewood had 8,500 abandoned and vacant lots, and of those 5,000 were abandoned residential lots (Figures 4.1 and 4.2). Given what members had learned at Green Healthy Neighborhoods meetings, R.A.G.E. partnered with CMAP to think through ways to address land use. During the summer months of 2013, R.A.G.E. members went block by block to survey the community about redeveloping vacant and abandoned spaces on their streets. Residents reported wanting community spaces and larger yards or open space for projects like public art and community gardens, and they expressed frustration with land use initiatives that were failing to take neighborhood constraints into consideration.[17]

Figure 4.1. Landscaper takes a break from his job maintaining vacant lots in Greater Englewood. Photo by Max Herman, August 1, 2011.

Figure 4.2. Abandoned and boarded-up house in Greater Englewood. Photo by Teresa Irene Gonzales, July 5, 2018.

R.A.G.E. members shared this information with CMAP and the Chicago Department of Housing and Economic Development.[18]

Out of these conversations emerged the Large Lot Program, through which the city allowed homeowners, block clubs, and local nonprofits to apply to purchase, for one dollar each, up to two city-owned vacant parcels on the purchaser's block.[19] To qualify, an applicant needed to not only own property on the block but also have paid all property taxes and have no other financial obligations to the city (including parking tickets). As an additional barrier to purchasing this land, residents could not easily identify which parcels of land were available. To ease the application process, R.A.G.E. member Douglas Hampton, a tall, wiry African American man with extensive training in computer coding, used his technical expertise to develop a website for the city where residents could input an address and identify any city-owned vacant land on the same block. Douglas elaborated, "It was really hard for residents to navigate the city website, so I contacted LISC [the Local Initiatives Support Corporation], and they used some grant money they had from the Knight Foundation, and we built a website" (Figure 4.3). Christine Jaspar, with Chicago's Department of Planning and Development, was impressed. "It totally blew my mind," she exclaimed. "It was perfect! It had all the open lots that existed in the area, and applicants could just click on an open lot, write down the information, and then upload an application. In a two-week period we got two thousand hits!"

In the first year of the Large Lot Program, the city received four hundred phone calls requesting more information and more than one hundred applications from Greater Englewood. At the end of 2014, 276 parcels had been sold. With the program's success, the city expanded the project to an additional thirty neighborhoods. R.A.G.E. members viewed the Large Lot Program as an opportunity for residents to invest in their community and take ownership of abandoned and blighted land. As Asiaha Butler, president of R.A.G.E., attested, "I do think having people [in Greater Englewood] take part in some of the land ownership, within their block, and for other folks to be involved. . . . It will get them that sense of ownership [and] spark some creative ideas, some beautiful ideas."[20] Similarly, Jordan Ng (who was, as mentioned earlier, a representative from Chicago's Department of Planning and Development) reflected, "When you look at a block, any vacant lot that's greened up

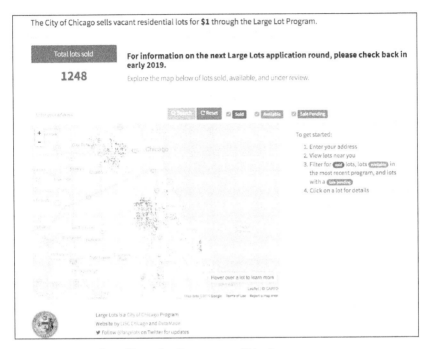

Figure 4.3. Screenshot of Large Lot Program as of March 2019.

improves the mentality of the entire block. It builds in that healthy tax base of the neighborhood; it improves the neighborhood overall. And it builds that sense of a community in an area that's been decimated."

Because the Large Lot Program is connected to Green Healthy Neighborhoods and the New Communities Program and is also supported by city offices, the Local Initiatives Support Corporation provided additional support, which included partnering with the Kresge Foundation to offer small grants to homeowners, ranging from $1,600 to $2,500, for thinking through creative place-making strategies for their parcels. As part of this effort, the Englewood lead agency, Teamwork Englewood, convened a team of experts to train residents on ways to develop their plots. The City of Chicago also worked with residents to transform the land. Over the summer of 2016, I sat with Jordan Ng and Christine Jaspar, another representative from the Department of Planning and Development, to discuss the evolution of these plans across neighborhoods in the New Communities Program. Christine and Jordan mentioned that they, along with R.A.G.E., were working with residents to develop the large lots, pairing residents with local developers to lease or develop the land into housing units or mixed retail spaces:

> CHRISTINE: Right now, what we want at this point is just for people to take on and maintain the lot so it doesn't look abandoned. So it's not a safety issue, and after five years they can sell it. Within the five-year period they can do whatever they want on the lot that's allowed by zoning.
>
> JORDAN: This program levels the playing field. It gives residents within the community the opportunity to then leverage that lot.

Although it was limited in scope, the Large Lot Program helped to build Black wealth. Once they had purchased the land, residents could develop it, within zoning regulations, as they wished. This included working with developers to build rental housing, creating a community garden, or expanding their own property lines. After the initial five-year waiting period, the large-lot owner could sell the lot for a profit at any time, with no penalty or fines owed to the city. By increasing resident ownership, the program could also curtail gentrification and displacement in a neighborhood with high rates of poverty and unemployment.

On the one hand, the Large Lot Program provided clear added gains to local residents and the city. On the other hand, it disproportionately benefited property owners who didn't necessarily live in the community, as Jordan highlighted: "[The Large Lot Program] is for people to make investments of their own. That's why we target homeowners. They already have a basic understanding of what it takes to maintain the property; you have to pay taxes, cut the grass, keep it clean. We look for people on the block because it's easier to care for a property when it's close to you." There were limited safeguards in place to ensure neighborhood residents benefitted from the program (for instance, a landlord who resided elsewhere could apply to the Large Lot Program). Additionally, only a small percentage of the residents in Englewood were homeowners during the period of my study, 68 percent of the population had no stake in the program because they lived in rental units and owned no property in the neighborhood. The Large Lot Program also transferred the burden of cleanup for these vacant parcels from the city, which had provided minimal maintenance, to local residents and homeowners.

Despite these challenges, the benefits of such collaboration are evident: because R.A.G.E. members worked with the Local Initiatives Support Corporation on this city-approved project, the Large Lot Program was implemented with relative ease and in a timely manner. R.A.G.E. members are respected by residents, and the group has a pulse on current issues in the community. Additionally, the Local Initiatives Support Corporation has friendly relationships with the city and was thus able to facilitate growing the project to include the expanded website and resident concerns. Furthermore, the intermediary provided additional support to ensure the program's success.

The Large Lot case thus demonstrates that local grassroots organizations can use their collective skepticism and their networks to partner with external actors and effectively leverage city support. R.A.G.E. used their collective skepticism of urban renewal processes to creatively address vacant land, influence land use policy in their community, and ensure that some residents directly benefitted from the program. In this way, as Ernie Jones suggested, R.A.G.E. members created their own sense of movement, had their own meetings, and invited city agencies into the decision-making process.

Not all redevelopment initiatives can claim such positive outcomes, however. In these neighborhoods, support for a project can depend on the city's broader interests and priorities. When these fail to align with community needs, however, grassroots organizations need to establish different kinds of partnerships. This is most evident in community responses to the railyard expansion that was linked to the CREATE projects. Here grassroots groups partnered with local agencies to confront city hall.

Chicago Region Environmental and Transportation Efficiency Program (CREATE)

The CREATE program established a $3.2 billion public-private effort to bring together the U.S. Department of Transportation, the State of Illinois, the City of Chicago, the commuter rail lines Amtrak and Metra, and national freight railroads such as Norfolk Southern and BNSF

Railway. At the time, it had received $426.55 million in federal grants, and with that funding it planned to increase rail infrastructure (tracks, switches, overpasses, underpasses, grade crossings, and signal systems) across the city.[21] Because these projects were publicly funded, project coordinators were required to hold public meetings and involve residents in the planning.

In Englewood, resident outreach for the CREATE projects included public forums and the creation of a community action group, with meetings attended by a representative from Norfolk Southern. To establish the community action group, Illinois Department of Transportation (IDOT) representatives Yvonne Daniels and Fae Jenkins compiled a list of stakeholders identified by church leaders, local aldermen, and the New Communities Program lead agencies. Yvonne described an effort extending beyond legal requirements for community input, to be as transparent as possible and to answer community questions.[22] During public meetings and meetings of the community action group, residents confirmed Yvonne's account.

These meetings provided residents with information, identified community stakeholders, and answered questions about the projects' implementation. Both the public forums and meetings of the community action group were heavily attended, with a minimum of forty residents each, along with representatives from local community organizations and from offices of local alderman and state representatives. As one community member recounted, representatives from CREATE had responded to all of her emails and phone calls in a timely manner, and staff members had made time for her to visit their office and further explain the CREATE projects and their effects for her, her home, and her community.

Representatives from Norfolk Southern often attended these meetings because of the connection between CREATE and the company's freight railyard expansion.[23] This expansion was an eighty-four-acre privately funded initiative that included the purchase of 105 city-owned vacant lots and 100 privately owned lots.[24] As a 2013 mayoral press release explained, "[The Norfolk Southern intermodal railyard site expansion will] reinforc[e] Chicago's transportation infrastructure . . . [and] help local manufacturers, distributors, and other companies that depend on cost-effective and convenient options to ship and receive goods. . . .

That means more efficiency for local businesses and more jobs for area residents." With mayoral and aldermanic support for the project, the city allocated funding, and in 2013, after Norfolk Southern had agreed to resident demands in Greater Englewood, the Chicago Plan Commission agreed to expand two tax increment financing districts so that the railway expansion could acquire the necessary funding.[25] As a result, although this was a private project, residents' property taxes were used to expand the freight yard. And despite residents' financial involvement in this way, community meetings were also neither required nor convened.

Partnering to Confront: Sustainable Englewood Initiatives and the Freight Yard Expansion

In 2010, as a response to the railyard expansion, John Paul Jones— Englewood resident, twenty-five-year community organizer, and transportation specialist—partnered with other residents and activists to create Sustainable Englewood Initiatives. This grassroots organization focused on the likely increase in air and noise pollution that would result from the Norfolk Southern freight yard expansion and on its other negative effects on homes and the community.

In a public notice published in the *Chicago Sun-Times* on August 6, 2012, Martin Cabrera Jr., the chairman of the Chicago Plan Commission, stated that Chicago would sell 104 parcels of public land in the Greater Englewood area to Norfolk Southern Railway for the railyard expansion project.[26] In response, and to mitigate power differentials between Englewood residents (many of whom were low-income and African American) and city hall in conversations, Sustainable Englewood partnered with Northwestern University's Law Clinic and relied on its technical expertise to apply environmental law and compile data on the ways that Norfolk Southern could reduce neighborhood pollution. Members of Sustainable Englewood held update meetings at the Englewood United Methodist Church, often including speakers from the community, legal counsel from Northwestern's Law Clinic, and representatives from the Environmental Protection Agency.

Many of the meetings were held during the day. Given high rates of violent crime and the popular portrayal of Englewood as crime-riddled, organizers were aware that many of their partners (particularly their legal advocates) might be unwilling to travel to the neighborhood at night. Daytime meetings sometimes restricted resident attendance; however, each meeting still drew twenty to thirty community members. Organizers also provided updates on their website and in the neighborhood digital newsletter, and they spoke about the railyard expansion at their churches and among friends and family.

Earlier efforts at advocacy on a different rail project, however, had led residents to mistrust this one. In 2006, residents of West Englewood, including John Paul Jones, had filed a class action lawsuit against CSX Transportation, another commercial railway in the city. The suit had claimed that high levels of noise, air, and traffic pollution came from the CSX freight yard. Residents wanted the company to limit operation to daytime and early evening, rather than operating twenty-four hours a day, and many complained of deteriorating homes (e.g., cracked walls, damaged ceilings) and increased illness (e.g., sleep deprivation, asthma) due to the movement of forty-ton steel containers at the site. Although CSX had acknowledged residents' complaints, the company claimed that cutting operating times would cost the company $500,000 per day, and a federal judge dismissed the lawsuit because the complaints had been filed with the wrong federal agency.[27] Notably, the city had negotiated a neighborhood investment agreement with CSX when the freight yard was first built, and the existence of this agreement meant that local aldermen were unable to advocate for changes in the company's practices.[28]

Although unconnected to Norfolk Southern or CREATE, this history had demonstrated the difficulties and obstacles that residents in Greater Englewood could encounter when attempting to confront commercial interests and the city, especially regarding this type of project. It also highlighted the inability of local aldermen to challenge city-backed development plans and their indifference as advocates for their constituents. These concerns, together with residents' perception of disrespect by Norfolk Southern at public meetings and the use of tax increment financing for the expansion, made this railyard expansion a relatively easy target for grassroots mobilizing. Given that they were challenging a city-approved, statewide redevelopment initiative, however, Sustainable Englewood Initiatives could not rely on the Local Initiatives Support Corporation, Teamwork Englewood, or even representatives from Green Healthy Neighborhoods for support or technical expertise.

As previously chronicled, IDOT representatives convened a resident community action group. Residents met monthly to discuss the potential impact of the commercial rail expansions. With IDOT controlling the dissemination of information regarding CREATE projects in this context, residents heard convincing arguments that supported rail expansion and that focused solely on the benefits for their community. Nonetheless, during town hall meetings, several residents expressed concerns about increased pollution, decreased property values, lack of local hiring mandates, and the proximity of the rail projects to local schools and parks. Although the CREATE and Norfolk Southern projects could clearly increase the city's commercial rail capacity, the costs of these gains, residents pointed out, could also be shifted to the residents of Greater Englewood.

Because projects under the CREATE umbrella are publicly funded through state and federal grants, they require this kind of community involvement throughout the planning process. As evidenced by the IDOT-run group, however, involvement is loosely defined and here included outreach to local churches, nonprofits, and politicians to identify active residents who would attend public meetings and join a community advisory group. When I asked about this process, one community member rolled his eyes and explained that, with this kind of selectivity, the city ensured that only people unlikely to challenge decisions were invited to public meetings. Still, the meetings remained open, and I was able to attend. There, I heard representatives from both IDOT and Norfolk Southern take a confrontational, sometimes evasive stance; this approach contrasted directly with how representatives from IDOT had portrayed their approach in conversations with me, claiming that they had gone "above and beyond" the legal requirement for community involvement.

A public meeting at St. Bernard Hospital illustrated these contradictions. There, a resident asked whether homeowners would be compensated for damages to property and for increased noise, air, and traffic pollution related to the expanded railyard. In response, representatives from Norfolk Southern first stated that these "subjective outcomes" were not the responsibility of the city, state, or rail lines, and they went on to state that because the railyard expansion was a private business endeavor, the project was not beholden to community interests. Such

Figure 4.4. Since 2011, Norfolk Southern Railway has been buying out and demolishing houses in this family's neighborhood to make way for a railyard expansion project. As of March 2016, this family was one of three homeowners who refused to sell. Photo by Max Herman, March 2016.

responses only reinforced residents' skepticism, and some refused to sell their homes to the freight company (Figure 4.4). Residents had, after all, encountered much resistance in aiming to affect decision making, requesting compensation, or requiring pollution controls after a project had been approved and finished. Then, at a "state of the neighborhood" address in the Twentieth Ward, Englewood Alderman Cochran added insult to injury. When asked about the expansion project's hiring mandates, he cited skill deficits that, he claimed, made local residents unemployable with CREATE or Norfolk Southern. With a 26.9 percent unemployment rate in Greater Englewood, this lack of aldermanic support for work opportunities was striking.

To challenge the freight yard expansion in the face of all of these barriers, members of Sustainable Englewood relied on a *partnering to confront* strategy. This strategy ensured that organizational members had access to technical expertise and legal advice regarding environmental pollution and enabled the group to effectively confront the city over blatant injustices. Unlike R.A.G.E., Sustainable Englewood hoped to disrupt, rather than support, plans for neighborhood redevelopment (Figures 4.5 and 4.6). Together with advocates from Northwestern's Law Clinic, fifteen residents attended the Chicago Plan Commission's meeting on August 15, 2013. There they highlighted the impending health risks of the expansion project and demanded both pollution controls and a clear outline of the ways in which the jobs from the Norfolk Southern expansion could benefit Greater Englewood residents and Black contractors.[29] Their lobbying delayed a vote on the expansion until Norfolk Southern could come to an agreement with residents. One month later, the company agreed to install pollution control equipment on thirty-six of thirty-eight trucks, to install clean engines or diesel filters on lift equipment, and to provide $2 million toward programming in Englewood. In addition, the City of Chicago agreed to fund the creation of green spaces on an abandoned elevated rail track.[30]

The actions taken by Sustainable Englewood Initiatives came about because of a lack of local political support and a history of development projects that had disenfranchised residents, causing increased pollution, redirected tax dollars, and inadequate employment opportunities in the wake of benefits for businesses, developers, and local politicians. Given the inclusion of the New Communities Program in these projects, the Local Initiatives Support Corporation could have mediated among residents, local politicians, and Norfolk Southern. Despite having become involved in the Large Lot Program, however, the corporation and the lead agencies took a hands-off approach in the work around the freight yard expansion. The local alderman's corresponding lack of support for local employment then exacerbated resident frustration.

Vast experience with these actors had generated the collective skepticism that spurred Sustainable Englewood's connection with Northwestern's Law Clinic. This partnership illustrates the value of networks of opportunity for negotiating tensions and the utility of partnering to confront inequitable development. Although they chose different partners due to variations in the context surrounding the projects to which they were responding, both Sustainable Englewood Initiatives and R.A.G.E. approached networking with local agencies to ensure that residents' needs were represented in new development initiatives. R.A.G.E. used their collective skepticism of urban renewal processes to strategically partner with the city and the Local Initiatives Support Corporation.

Fact Sheet: Diesel Pollution in Chicago

Chicago is a national hub for transportation. Diesel engines power many of the heavy-duty trucks, locomotives, construction equipment and railyard equipment that dot our landscape. Most of these vehicles do not have state-of-the-art pollution controls that can filter their exhaust. Without such protections, a toxic mixture of soot and gases is harming Chicagoans — particularly those who live near highways, railyards and intermodal facilities. There is a solution. You can help.

Diesel Engines in Chicago. Our city is a national hub for freight transportation, with rail yards, arterial highways, intermodal freight centers and warehouses. While this provides a huge benefit to the local economy, the health of Chicagoans also suffers.

Diesel engines power numerous types of equipment, including heavy-duty trucks, locomotives, construction equipment and rail yard equipment like cranes. If these diesel engines do not have state-of-the-art pollution controls (and many do not), their exhaust contains a toxic mixture of tiny soot particles and gases. This mixture absorbs metals and toxic gases in the exhaust and delivers them to your lungs.

Health Risks. Diesel soot contributes to an estimated 21,000 deaths in America every year. Recently, medical researchers have begun to uncover evidence that diesel pollution can cause fatal diseases, such as cancer, stroke and heart attacks — as well as worsen asthma.

Everyone in the region is at risk from this kind of diesel pollution. However, health professionals worry in particular about those living and working in close proximity to areas where diesel engines are concentrated. Such high numbers of diesel engines are found on major highways and arterial roads, at intermodal facilities and at large construction projects.

Solution. The good news is that this problem has a very achievable solution. Engineers have developed filters that can clean up diesel engine exhaust. All trucks and other diesel vehicles need these filters. In addition, common sense measures such as limiting idling, managing traffic better, and creating "buffer zones" between dense diesel pollution and residential areas can go a long way toward making Chicago's air safer to breath.

Take Action At http://bit.ly/eDiesel

Figure 4.5. Sustainable Englewood Initiatives fact sheet regarding diesel pollution in Chicago.

Community Demands

1) **Quality of life and Public Health**
   - **Environmental concerns, air quality mitigation, and health testing:** Focusing on diesel air pollution and lead contamination.
   - **Mitigation of structural damage to roads, sidewalks and homes:** Creation of a fund for community to repair damage from increased truck traffic.
   - **Noise reduction/mitigation**
2) **High-quality green space:** Development of high-quality recreational and green space in the community possibly including walking and bike trails.
   - New ERA Trail: Transfer land needed for the trail to the city or Forest Preserve District; obtain initial engineering and design plans; fund for some part of development into greenway, walking/biking trails; use Bloomingdale Trail as a model.
   - Remediation of impacts to parks located near the expanded 47th Street Terminal.
3) **Buffer zones and fostering community goals for local economic development**

Figure 4.6. Sustainable Englewood Initiatives community demands.

Echoing Hilary's statement in the opening of this chapter, R.A.G.E. was skeptical of the motives for this support; however, they also knew that they needed the city and the Local Initiatives Support Corporation for the Large Lot Program to be successful. In other contexts, however, as described in the next section, yet another form of partnering was necessary to get the job done.

Partnering with a Broad Network: LVEJO and the Park

Within Little Village, aside from the New Communities Program, there were not any additional large-scale redevelopment initiatives for the area to address. Nevertheless, as illustrated in the next section, grassroots groups still strategically used networks of opportunity to ensure that key strategies in the quality-of-life plans were implemented and to oversee the environmental cleanup of a contaminated area. In this case, activists *partnered with a broad-based coalition* to pressure the Environmental Protection Agency and the city to remediate a highly contaminated superfund site and create a new park in the neighborhood.

The Park

Throughout the New Communities Program's quality-of-life planning that occurred in Little Village from 2003 to 2005, residents highlighted their desire for additional park space in their densely populated community. In 2005, when the final quality-of-life report was published, the need for a park was one of the neighborhood's top three development projects.

The quality-of-life plan stated that the lead agency and its partners would work to "expand access to parks and open space by improving facilities and creating a large new park."[31] The city then identified two sites as potential locations: a high-traffic, asbestos-contaminated former trade school and a highly contaminated, postindustrial superfund site. Both areas required environmental cleanup, but the postindustrial site also required extensive remediation, as it had a seventy-year history of manufacturing pollutants such as coal, tar, asphalt, and driveway sealer.[32] The site of the former trade school, which did not require such remediation, was therefore identified as the future site of the park. The initial time frame for creation of the park was two to five years, and the plan cited leads on the project that included Enlace (the lead agency), a violence prevention group, Twenty-Second Ward Alderman Muñoz's office, and a local Catholic church.[33] With the backing of the Local Initiatives Support Corporation and the aldermanic office, the creation of the park seemed inevitable.[34]

Despite this appearance of support, however, the Local Initiatives Support Corporation informed Enlace in 2006 that creating a park in Little Village was opposed by Mayor Richard M. Daley, the Park District, and the city administration, which had also identified the highly contaminated postindustrial site as the only location available for it (Figure 4.7).[35] As a result, regarding continued work on the park, Enlace was informed by corporation staff that "there [would be] a cost to that." When I asked a local community activist about the city's reasons

Figure 4.7. A composite view of the cleanup site, from Twenty-Seventh Street on the right all the way to Thirty-First Street on the left. Photo by Jay Dunn, August 25, 2009.

for opposing the park, I was told, "I honestly don't know. But my guess is money; the city just doesn't want to spend that kind of cash here. But they'll spend it to create Maggie Daley Park," which was a centrally located downtown development named after Mayor Richard M. Daley's deceased wife that opened near several tourist attractions in 2014.[36]

Partnering with a Broad Network: LVEJO

To placate residents, who were upset about the bait and switch, and to remain on friendly terms with the city and the Local Initiatives Support Corporation, the lead agency, Enlace, transferred ownership of the park project to a small, grassroots organization, the Little Village Environmental Justice Organization (LVEJO). However, as with Sustainable Englewood Initiatives, this change rendered inaccessible any funds, technical expertise, or political connections that had been available for the park project through the New Communities Program. At this point, LVEJO lacked the internal capacity to advocate for the park or create new development plans, but its organizers did know how to network and how to mobilize residents. The organization accomplished these aims through holding public land use meetings, activating relational ties, and meeting with city officials.

Given the loss of resources associated with the New Communities Program, the remediation process would have taken much longer had LVEJO not been willing to identify a need and find help outside the neighborhood. As with the freight yard expansion in Greater Englewood, Little Village's grassroots organizations needed to partner with exogenous groups to ensure that redevelopment plans were equitable.

Unlike the networks in Greater Englewood, however, these partnerships extended well beyond the city, to encompass a range of environmental organizations, such as the Green Club, Environmental Protection Agency (EPA), Sierra Club, Chicago-based Environmental Law and Policy Center, and Keepers of the Mountain, a group of Appalachian environmentalists. This broad coalition of network members provided LVEJO with access to information, specialized skills, and successful strategies for achieving their goals. The organization relied on these external actors for technical assistance but managed not to allow them to dictate its agenda or define community needs. When I spoke with LVEJO's Clean Power community organizer, who had joined the organization as a teenage volunteer, he expressed frustration that some people considered reliance on external help a sign that LVEJO had been co-opted or had engaged in poverty pimping: "If there had been an environmental lawyer in Little Village, we would have used them, you know. But there wasn't! What are we supposed to do, wait another ten years to see if maybe the initiative would have been successful? No, we had an opportunity to talk with people who know the legal system and strategize so that we could win. That's not co-optation."[37] Working with experts is a central component of networks of opportunity. Rather than *keeping it real* and waiting for local expertise to arise, similar to Sustainable Englewood, LVEJO strategically identified partners who could help advance the organization's goals and, ultimately, benefit the larger community.

Before planning the park, members of LVEJO had gone door to door to ask area residents about their thoughts for a site. Not only did this outreach mobilize residents, but it also revealed the detrimental impact of the city's neglect in this part of the neighborhood. Mario Rivera, a twenty-year-old organizer with LVEJO, talked about the importance of this grassroots organizing:

> Do you know about the park? The development of that is how I see accommodating all needs. That part [of the neighborhood, on the Southeastern Side] isn't only intellectually and emotionally neglected, it's physically neglected as well. You go in and some streets are crappy; some streets don't even have sidewalks or whatever. Some roads aren't even paved. . . . So we go in, and we start talking to residents, and they were like "You sure

you want a park here?" And we were like "Yeah why not?!" . . . and they were like "Cool, okay, come check out our houses when it floods." Then we learned about other issues going on in that part of the neighborhood.

Through these conversations, LVEJO learned that 170 neighborhood homes had been contaminated by run-off water from the designated park site. Recounting this revelation, Mario was both furious and frustrated:

> They told us about how their basements would flood and how they would get rashes . . . where the water would touch. . . . It was crazy, like you live in the U.S.; you live in Chicago; this shouldn't be happening you know? Nobody should be going through this, . . . and you know what? People were scared that they would go to a doctor one day and they would be diagnosed with cancer or something. So we put the park thing on hold and were like let's fix this first.

Through LVEJO's work on advocating for a park in an "intellectually, emotionally, and physically" neglected area of the neighborhood, the organization was able to uncover long-term environmental neglect and abuse. Residents knew that the land was contaminated but did not know who was responsible for it or how to go about getting the land cleaned.

In conversation with area residents and in researching the site, LVEJO learned that the EPA had found pollution there dating back to 1989 and had informed the public in 1997 that the site had been regraded to improve drainage (and thus lead to lower pollution).[38] Yet in 2006, after complaints made by LVEJO members and local residents, the EPA again tested soil samples and discovered high levels of pollution, both at the potential park site and in surrounding homes.[39] Although the agency had found contaminated soil in 1989, had heard resident complaints in 1996 and 2006, and had agreed to hold the landowner accountable, an approved plan for soil cleanup appeared only in 2008. In the intervening years, members of LVEJO and local residents continued calling, questioning, videotaping illegal dumping at the site, and reporting pollution to the EPA and the city.

Describing the legal process for site remediation, the former LVEJO park organizer Naila Sanchez explained, "It was crazy because I mean, the EPA didn't even want to clean it to their own standards. We had to secretly film illegal dumping and constantly monitor what was happening with the site, because the EPA just wouldn't engage." The EPA's continued negligence in overseeing remediation underlines the challenges that community groups confront when attempting to remedy the inequalities of past development policies, many of which have allowed for the demise of poor communities and promoted environmental racism. Environmental scholars highlight the prevalence and impact of environmental pollution on Black, Indigenous, Latina/o/x, immigrant, and impoverished communities across the United States.[40] Recent scholarship reveals that Black and Latina/o/x populations disproportionately live near polluting industries and breathe in pollutants overwhelmingly generated by White consumption. The result is a "pollution burden" that is rarely rectified.[41]

Once cleanup finally started in 2009, LVEJO monitored it, as members feared the EPA and the city were failing to perform due diligence (given the slow pace of remediation and the history of neglect) and was shifting the cost of cleanup to the taxpayers rather than holding the landowner accountable.[42] As a result, despite initial difficulties, cleanup for both the postindustrial site and residents' homes was completed in 2009, and the Chicago Park District finally acquired the future park site in 2012.

Even before this point, though, LVEJO worked to engage Little Village residents, especially those closest to the site, in planning the park (Figures 4.8, 4.9, and 4.10). Meetings, known in local economic development as charrettes, were held over the course of a year at various venues, such as schools, churches, and the library.[43] At a meeting held in February 2010, for example, twenty mothers came together over coffee and *pan dulce* to discuss their ideal park.[44] Some of the ideas included a petting zoo, a space for year-round sports, and an athletics space that could accommodate group classes. A major component of the park project included encouraging young people to creatively and strategically reimagine the abandoned site. In November 2010, residents and LVEJO members appeared at a Chicago Park District board meeting to outline their Parks Program Layout for the site; slated to cost $450 million, the park would include an urban farm, playgrounds, sports fields, an amphitheater, and a community center.[45] The plan, which grew out of the year of meetings, was illustrated using a 3D model created by a LVEJO intern from the Art Institute of Chicago.[46]

Figure 4.8. Youth coordinator shows participants in a local leadership program a park plan for the site, a possible home for much-needed open space. Photo by Jay Dunn, August 25, 2009.

Figure 4.9. A longtime resident of Little Village and board member of LVEJO points out changes to the park plan. Photo by Jay Dunn, August 25, 2009.

Figure 4.10. Youth activist holding park proposals near the cleanup site in Little Village. Photo by Jay Dunn, August 25, 2009.

In the end, the plans the community had presented were taken into consideration, and the community's influence was evident when the park opened in December 2014.[47] At 21.5 acres, it included five athletic fields, a skate park, basketball courts, community gardens, a large playground, a multiuse trail, and picnic and lounging areas. Despite this influence, however, and involvement of well-meaning local and national organizations, the Park District had hired an external contractor to design the park, and according to Naila, neither LVEJO nor community residents were consulted by either the Park District or the contractor during development. Both the Park District decision to disengage from residents during the final planning phases and the relocation of the park to the postindustrial site highlight the power of local government in making final development decisions, which often did not align with what was best for the local community.

The community effectively applied collective skepticism as a tactical tool here while engaging the expertise of external agents in a network of opportunity, allowing LVEJO to move beyond feelings of apathetic mistrust where residents and community groups completely disengage due to histories of mistreatment and dispossession. As mentioned earlier, due to a lack of city support and because Enlace had stepped back from involvement in creating the park, the Local Initiatives Support Corporation was unwilling to provide any aid. This inaction highlights the added barriers that political and organizational boundaries present, both to the lead agencies and to community groups unaffiliated with the New Communities Program. These barriers, coupled with the EPA's negligence in overseeing the remediation process, compounded the challenges that community groups confront when attempting to remedy the effects of unequal development policies that have allowed air and land pollution in poor communities. At the same time, the park project illustrates the importance of having local residents and community groups advocate for development and ensure that legal mandates are followed and that local politicians and corporations are held accountable. Trusting in government and nonprofits would not have led to the same oversight and regulation of the cleanup process. Yet LVEJO used collective skepticism to engage in a broad network that could help them address immediate concerns—such as ground pollution—and also tactically plan for long-term goals to ensure the success of the Little Village park.

Conclusion

The Large Lot Program, the freight yard initiative, and the public park project were accomplished through the strategic networking of neighborhood grassroots organizations—specifically R.A.G.E., Sustainable Englewood, and LVEJO. In each case, rather than trusting that the Local Initiatives Support Corporation, the New Communities Program, or the city would adequately address resident concerns (e.g., pollution, green spaces, and abandoned property), these grassroots groups developed other partnering strategies. They understood the complex ways that interorganizational trust is linked to privilege and power. As a result, they relied on networks of opportunity—in which key staff collaborated with local activists, neighborhood groups, and experts from local and national organizations—for skills, training, and feedback on their work. Depending on these external relationships to accomplish their goals, these organizations forged partnerships that were mutually beneficial and relationships that were built upon mutual goals. Community efforts thus ensured that community voices would be heard.

In building these different kinds of partnerships, these groups effectively harnessed collective skepticism of city processes, building networks with relevant actors to support resident-focused initiatives. These relationships are distinct from the commonly touted system of overt interorganizational trust and dependence, in which a community organization is beholden to a partner for operating funds, political or economic clout, or access to some other resource. Instead, as connections forged for a narrower purpose, these external relationships, which were tempered with collective skepticism, presented less risk for co-optation. Emerging here instead was a mutual dependence in which organizational partners gained access to resources—perhaps course credits, involvement in a green campaign, or good public relations with poor communities—while grassroots organizations gained valuable, often free access to skilled labor and innovative ideas.[48] By partnering with external organizations in this way, these community groups in Chicago developed strategies to limit the risk that the Local Initiatives Support Corporation or the lead agencies would monopolize organizational or redevelopment space.

Additionally, creating such networks of opportunity allowed groups like R.A.G.E., Sustainable Englewood Initiative, and LVEJO to move beyond models of "keeping it real" and "poverty pimping" and into a framework of *àse* in order to redress a legacy of social exclusion that disenfranchises the poor and communities of color. This process highlights a shift away from hyper-focused social service programming, which too often characterizes poverty as personal failure. R.A.G.E., Sustainable Englewood Initiative, and LVEJO take a different approach: they train and empower local residents to strategically build coalitions in order to ensure more socially just development and wealth-building projects.

As illustrated in these examples, rather than focusing on the language of trust (which too often conceals power inequities), these grassroots organizations engaged in tactical partnerships to achieve specific goals. In the conclusion I ask us to reconsider the value of trust and, drawing on the work of grassroots organizing in Black and Mexican Chicago, to outline new ways of engaging residents and improving resident-led inclusion within redevelopment.

Conclusion

What's Trust Got to Do with It?

If it doesn't add value to some of the most challenged communities in the city of Chicago, then why bother?
—Naila Sanchez, 2014

Sometimes when you bring in these cure-alls or these we're-
going-to-fix-its, it decentralizes what's already been happening in a way. All of a sudden the community groups are not
the important agencies anymore, and residents stop going to
them. Now residents and the city start going to LISC [the
Local Initiatives Support Corporation] as the mothership.
—Ernie Jones, 2012

As with many policy initiatives, the New Communities Program was
influenced by previous efforts at urban renewal to address inner-city
poverty and decay. As part of this program, the Local Initiatives Support Corporation used an approach that was similar to those used in
earlier efforts—that is, it favored traditional community development
practices, which do not challenge existing power structures. The crux
of the initiative was to implement urban development through sound
research, relationship building, public-private partnerships, and holistic
redevelopment plans. In this aim, it succeeded: by acting as intermediary
between city officials and local nonprofits in sixteen neighborhoods, the
organization developed a method and common framework for its clients.

The main mechanism by which the New Communities Program operated was the neighborhood quality-of-life plan. These plans provided
blueprints for possible redevelopment in each neighborhood, brought
residents together to provide input on the reports, and attempted to create a unified redevelopment vision for each community. At the same

time, the process of creating these plans revealed areas for redevelopment that fell outside the New Communities purview. For instance, areas along Chicago's Southeast corridor were identified as ideal for an agricultural district, and those areas became the Green Healthy Neighborhoods; it also identified as a priority the expansion of commercial mass transit, which aligned with the existing Chicago Region Environmental and Transportation Efficiency Program (CREATE).

Although no organization conducted door-to-door data collection to ensure broader, more representative feedback for these two initiatives, many residents highlighted concerns about them at public meetings. For example, residents were frustrated that the Local Initiatives Support Corporation took an active role in supporting the city's Green Healthy Neighborhoods project but that its support did not extend to local community organizations struggling against corporate and political elites in achieving the goals of this project. However, that distinction was central to the corporation's approach—the organization avoided offering clear and public support for these groups because doing so could have jeopardized its role as intermediary between elites and the nonprofit professionals in their target neighborhoods.[1] As a result, it was more difficult to garner support for the kind of work residents wanted to focus on.

Ultimately, all of the projects outlined in the final neighborhood quality-of-life reports did stem from resident feedback and involvement. The planning incorrectly assumed, however, that resident input was the same as resident consensus; as this book has shown, participating neighborhoods offered no unified "resident voice," and there was no space in the planning process to field any variety in resident desires. Instead, views of redevelopment flowed from a select few residents, who were typically hand-picked by urban elites to attend community meetings because they were unlikely to challenge the underlying power structure. As a result, when the redevelopment projects were then implemented, few mechanisms were available to ensure that local residents would truly benefit from them.

New Communities Program as a Place-Based Socializing Project

Using such efficient, professional intermediaries for redevelopment and urban renewal campaigns reflects the neoliberal tenets of privatization that favor the growth model of development and further shields the government from culpability—as the nonprofit sector is tasked with providing public goods and services. The process streamlines development, works to build consensus among residents, and supports a singular vision for the city—all of which sounds positive but, as explained in earlier chapters, can result in changes that do not truly benefit the local population. The New Communities Program operated within this realm, with the Local Initiatives Support Corporation as a nonprofit intermediary that spanned philanthropy, government, and community-based organizations. Here lies the focus on building relationships and networks of trust, which raise residents' expectations that city and community groups will honor their wishes but don't necessarily deliver on those expectations. The process also reaffirms experts, foundations, and local nonprofits as agents responsible for neighborhood redevelopment, with little regard for the expertise and desires of residents. In this context, nonprofits—whether national intermediaries or community organizations—remain constrained, both by their funders and by the government, in the changes on behalf of which they can advocate.

Although this approach meant that the Local Initiatives Support Corporation often promoted the desires of urban elites over the concerns of local residents, the New Communities Program also provided some benefits to the communities. It promoted a comprehensive, holistic approach to "add value to some of the most challenged communities," as Naila Sanchez, a onetime Little Village organizer, explained. Each of the sixteen neighborhoods experienced substantial gains in resources, including more businesses, more housing and greater rates of home ownership, declines in housing and commercial vacancies, new or expanded green spaces, newly created city-backed nonprofits, and inclusion in other public and private initiatives. Locals interested in neighborhood development writ large were encouraged to partner with the intermediary rather than act as adversaries. Even though several neighborhood activists and grassroots organizations did challenge the New Communities Program and were skeptical of the process, they, too, worked on issues raised by residents during the extensive quality-of-life planning.

Benefits also flowed to the lead agencies and the Local Initiatives Support Corporation. Emphasizing relationship building between philanthropy and city officials, the organization offered lead agencies legitimacy, access to city-level decision makers, and funds for development projects. At the center of these gains, the corporation positioned itself as the foremost national expert in community development.

This comprehensive neighborhood approach to poverty and urban redevelopment could work: it can, at least in theory, provide an opportunity to address structural barriers to success for marginalized and historically oppressed populations. A focus on a specific geographic space, such as a neighborhood, also allows funders and city officials to redirect resources to historically neglected areas.[2]

In practice, however, neighborhood-focused initiatives in communities of color rarely account for local needs and often equate the people who live in neglected areas with their denigrated conditions. Black and Brown residents of decayed urban neighborhoods thus come to be seen as morally decayed themselves, and initiatives risk perpetuating negative stereotypes of the "inner city" and pathologizing residents of color, regardless of residence or class background. Moreover, neighborhood approaches seek to fix systemic issues through a micro lens and so may miss broader problems. For example, the New Communities Program addressed poverty in Greater Englewood and Little Village but not its causes, including local disinvestment in communities of color. This effort therefore changed the physical environment and provided social services without changing the conditions that perpetuate urban poverty. If development spurs displacement, for instance, impoverished residents must find work, housing, and education elsewhere, thus creating a cascade of poverty-driven mobility.

In local economic development, this inaccurate vision frames urban planning and guides elites' expectations for resident involvement. Oftentimes, this logic assumes that residents from historically oppressed populations lack agency and are "passive [and powerless] objects requiring intervention" by expert practitioners.[3] Rather than incorporating them as true collaborators, experts follow a paternalistic model, similar to Isabel's as discussed in chapter 3, that simply informs low-income and Black and Latina/o/x residents of new development initiatives.

In Chicago, where two-thirds of residents identify as either Black and/or Latina/o/x and the Latina/o/x population is steadily increasing, this approach strategically incorporates key Blacks and Latinas/os/ xs into a vision of the city that aligns with White political elites while disenfranchising most Black and Latina/o/x residents. Neighborhood groups that don't subscribe to this vision can then be dismissed as inefficient, unprofessional, or naïve.

Who Are the Experts?

Several New Communities Program reports highlight relationships, coalition building, and local assets in impoverished communities. Yet a language of relationship building—through building trust with friendly urban elites—conveys much of the program's story. This approach favors development from above rather than from below. Partner agencies in the neighborhoods are expected to implement the program; socialize themselves to businesslike, professional modes of behavior; and trust in the Local Initiatives Support Corporation's method of redevelopment. In marginalized communities, this neighborhood redevelopment policy perpetuates strategies that include poor residents only peripherally in decision making. Additionally, successful initiatives that resident-led community groups conduct without support from the program are, in turn, folded into the program's broader success story. Redevelopment thus remains driven, top down, by experts and plans, and benefits accrue to those elites, not to the community.

Another challenge with making professional nonprofits the vanguard of neighborhood redevelopment and treating them as the primary experts is that doing so minimizes the innovative ideas that arise outside these organizations. As a result, neighborhood-based programs too often fall victim to the whims of funders and elected officials, and local nonprofits are unable to sustain those programs (as with the Smart Communities project).

The New Communities place-based approach—coupled with the language of social capital and trust and with a self-help, asset-based model of development—further places the onus on residents of marginalized communities, rather than the government, to address deep structures of inequality. These conditions absolve the state of accountability while also making it more difficult for the neighborhood to achieve its goals.

In its focus on social services and relationship building, and because of its unwillingness to challenge the city, the New Communities Program attempted to eradicate the pathologies of the poor while supporting an elite urban vision. Learning from urban renewal's mistakes, in the 1950s urban planners and development elites no longer used the language of deficiency or excluded locals from decision making; rather, they employed celebratory language that honored the gifts and special skills of local residents. Consistent with principles of asset-based community development, which focuses on building relationships and working collaboratively to address social ills, development elites framed their projects as resident focused. Although the changes were appropriate, however, they were not accompanied by true investment in what the community members wanted. Additionally, the celebrated assets were only those that fit the larger municipal vision, and they generally extended to only a select, "worthy" few.

Essentially, the New Communities Program instituted a hybrid model of local economic development that used asset-based language to include residents but relied on technocratic experts, political whims, and growth-based market forces for final decisions rather than on the local community. I do not mean to imply that technical expertise is not needed; of course it is. However, technical expertise and large-scale redevelopment plans must also consider the everyday realities of local residents. For example, although in a vacuum it might seem cost-effective to close the local post office or limit public transportation, urban redevelopers and elected officials must also consider the impact of these decisions on residents' lives and the local culture. Taken together, technical expertise regarding redevelopment and residents' expertise regarding their lived realities can complement each other. Truly collaborating with locals in redevelopment initiatives increases residents' ownership and acceptance of new developments and can work to diminish the potential for resident displacement and increase the quality of life for all residents.

Part of the challenge, however, was that funding entities and local politicians often dismissed more impactful, smaller-scale projects in favor of more flashy large-scale ones. Although, the New Communities Program in some ways promoted the involvement of residents in development decisions and the strengthening of relationships, when working with local groups the program actually supported a top-down vision of the city that kept poor residents at arm's length. The collaboration it promoted therefore failed to address issues of social injustice, while simultaneously concealing the various ways that interorganizational trust relationships masked inequalities.

In such top-down initiatives, Black and Latina/o/x residents were thus left to themselves to address pressing concerns and then blamed if those concerns weren't adequately addressed. Should city hall choose to close local schools, for example, residents would need to either fight to retain them or open their own schools. Should city hall refuse to pave roads or provide adequate garbage removal, members of marginalized groups would have to pressure city officials to provide such basic city services. If residents did not act and as a result garbage was strewn about or children lacked reading skills, that lack of state services still went unchallenged. Poor residents of color were then blamed for the decayed conditions of their neighborhoods, their employment status, and their children's lack of education.

In contrast, as I witnessed in Greater Englewood and Little Village, redevelopment processes from below can enhance resident ownership and civic participation and can improve overall quality of life.[4] Focused less on social capital and trust, although they are present, development from below can bring people together to expand democracy.[5] Residents involved in the Little Village park project and in the Greater Englewood Large Lot Program and railyard initiative achieved direct benefits from their sustained involvement through design input, land ownership, and cleanup of contaminated soil. In Chicago, therefore, strong civil society and grassroots organizations were necessary to ensure that development projects equitably benefited all residents.[6]

Trust as a One-Way Street

A central goal of local economic development is to build trust among poor residents. To address issues of mistrust, scholars and urban policy makers have latched onto the idea of building social capital (through expanded networks) and opening access to planning processes, targeted funds, and technical expertise. Additionally, building relationships between neighborhood-level groups and city agencies is meant to expand residents' awareness of city government and enhance their trust in municipal decisions. Trust in this context, however, is typically linear and rarely reciprocal. With the New Communities Program, for example, residents were expected to trust the state, the process, and the Local Initiatives Support Corporation but were extended little trust in return.

Such processes further disenfranchise communities of color, which are regularly expected and encouraged to trust the state, despite their experience and consequent misgivings.

In building relationships with such one-way trust, the Local Initiatives Support Corporation promoted the idea that the effects of poverty are equal to its causes. Yet they could have used the New Communities Program as an opportunity to highlight the underlying social inequalities that lead to poverty. Their purposeful failure to do so situated the corporation as an intermediary that was friendly to city officials who were uninterested in addressing ongoing urban inequalities. It also centered social services as the solution to human development, locked low-income residents into a client relationship with funders and the city, and allowed the city to continue to blame poor residents for their decayed neighborhoods. As a senior corporation official stated, residents and local nonprofits are expected to lift themselves up by their proverbial bootstraps: "We're not responsible, and we don't have to hold your hand. It's up to the lead agencies to collaborate and to implement an efficient and sustainable project."

Here the Local Initiatives Support Corporation did not view itself as responsible for the failures of the lead agencies designated as partners and provided no additional support for projects that were not aligned with the city's goals for redevelopment. There is an ongoing imbalance in these relationships. Public officials and development experts expect residents' trust and buy-in for their development projects, but they do not respond in kind—they have the power to provide only the support they deem necessary.

Collective Skepticism as Rational Response

As explained earlier, focusing on building relationships of trust in impoverished communities of color assumes a simplistic approach to development that implies that poor people of color should trust the very institutions that contribute to the conditions of racialized poverty. This approach fails to account for inherently unequal power relations between elites (including policy makers) and poor, overwhelmingly Black and Latina/o/x residents who have limited influence in urban redevelopment initiatives. For example, both Greater Englewood and

Little Village had experienced urban disinvestment, through school closures, underfunding of public education, lack of public services, and environmental racism. As a result, these low-income Black and Latina/o/x residents of Chicago had little reason to trust city hall, even when the New Communities Program encouraged them to do so.

Arguments for building trust in the processes of community development overlook the histories of exclusion that impoverished communities of color have experienced in urban settings. Indeed, to expect marginalized populations to ignore their lived histories of oppression risks perpetuating their exclusion when experience logically tells them to mistrust urban development policies. It is eminently reasonable for Black and Latina/o/x residents from low-income communities to be skeptical of any new plans for urban renewal. Rather than causing them to disengage from city processes, however, such mistrust—through collective skepticism—can be harnessed and used strategically to their advantage.

Grassroots organizations strategically harnessed collective skepticism by engaging resident mistrust of city process and acknowledging their histories of dispossession. In Chicago, for example, community leaders affiliated with Sustainable Englewood Initiatives, R.A.G.E., and LVEJO worked to create new avenues for residents to become involved in development decisions in their respective communities. To accomplish this new level of engagement, they built temporary goal-focused networks of opportunity that promoted connection and collaboration among neighborhood residents, and they approached public officials with well-researched data, development plans, and community needs. Through these actions, residents and community groups pressured corporations and city politicians to create plans that would truly benefit them. Their use of collective skepticism thus had clear benefits for local residents as well as for the city, even though their efforts also led to redevelopment plans that did not fully align with the city's agenda. As scholars have argued, redevelopment plans that truly benefit all populations must view residents—not only urban elites—as both owners and beneficiaries, and collective skepticism is a tool residents can use to ensure that happens.[7]

Students, scholars, and practitioners of community development, therefore, have to ask some pointed questions of themselves. In planning, designing, or implementing projects, are they unwittingly replicating social inequities? Local economic development focuses on geographic location but is also a commitment to the people of a place. Is that focus on development of people overly skewed toward social services? Does a focus on human development—which addresses violence, homelessness, drug addiction, and low education and employment rates—conflate the causes with the effects of poverty? Do redevelopment projects, whether urban or rural, overly focus on cosmetic physical redevelopment? Does human development through social services miss the underlying "root causes" that continue the cycles of poverty that community development claims but often fails to address?

It's true that providing money for beautification projects can transform decayed and blighted spaces. Similarly, providing after-school programming for students, workforce development for adults, and violence prevention and peace initiatives for community members can improve their life chances and overall quality of life. This critique is not to demean those endeavors. These initiatives alone, however, fail to address structural barriers to economic and social equality, particularly for marginalized populations. Community development needs to address these issues too. Despite calls for efficiency and austerity, no single model or method of redevelopment will accomplish this goal—what works in one neighborhood, town, city, or state may not work in another. Furthermore, advocating for trust does not take into consideration unequal power relations, nor does it attempt to redress histories of race- and class-based exclusion from development processes. Examples from grassroots organizing—as demonstrated by R.A.G.E., LVEJO, and Sustainable Englewood Initiatives—reveal locally based initiatives rooted in local cultures, histories, and economies that provide sustainable and adaptable models.

An Expansive Organizational Field

As scholars of poverty and local economic development highlight and as has been discussed at length here, campaigns for neighborhood redevelopment too often ignore the desires of low-income residents.[8] Furthermore, some community development scholars have decried the power differentials in interorganizational networks, claiming that these networks deprive residents of their civic voices.[9] The residents, lead agencies, and grassroots groups in Greater Englewood and Little Village, however, provide us with another story. Yes, community groups may lose a degree of autonomy and may even be co-opted. Yes, they may transform their missions to align better with city officials' expectations. These outcomes, however, are neither all-encompassing nor characteristic of all community organizations.

Community groups and their approaches to neighborhood redevelopment are as varied as the individuals who compose them. While their actions may be not always align, these organizations can provide complementary—if contradictory—strategies for ensuring residents benefit from citywide initiatives. The New Communities lead agencies strategically aligned with the Local Initiatives Support Corporation's process and focused primarily on individually targeted social services. In contrast, Sustainable Englewood, LVEJO, and R.A.G.E. engaged in leadership development that reached beyond individual transformation. These organizations incorporated residents' voices, bodies, and ideas into their action plans. Their members focused on both advancing residents' skill sets and transforming larger structural inequities. In these organizations, leadership development provided skills building, empowerment, and self-confidence while also creating opportunities for personal development.[10] They deployed collective skepticism strategically to address gaps in the New Communities Program's quality-of-life plans. Ultimately, the combined focus of the program's lead agencies and these grassroots organizations offered more holistic, expansive neighborhood redevelopment, for both people and physical spaces.

Given the pervasive language of trust in organizational analysis, collective skepticism may have other applications as well. For me, one came to mind in an ad hoc faculty meeting where colleagues were discussing ways to expand community engagement between university faculty and partners in the city and local neighborhoods. During the conversation, I was surprised to hear several colleagues highlight trust building between the university and its potential partners. I certainly recognized the university's civic responsibility to local residents and organizations—what struck me, however, was the emphasis on trust with little acknowledgment of the underlying institutional power dynamics. The university's experts could help local entities, I heard expressed, if they needed assistance or research on some social issue. To offer this help, my colleagues noted, the university must reach out to local organizations, so that community partners would learn to trust the university.

As with development, this use of the language of trust intuitively makes sense. As I asked at the outset of this book, how are we to get anything done if we don't trust? Yet for me, this final example highlighted the way that the good-natured language of trust insidiously encourages engagement without interrogating the social dynamics and power differentials inherent to these relationships. During this conversation there was no discussion of how this trust might benefit our own agendas—whether for research, good public relations, or something else. And there was no discussion of the steps we might take to ensure true collaborative approaches to local issues or to hold ourselves accountable to local concerns. If locals and area nonprofits don't trust the university (or government officials, local industries, news media outlets, etc.), surely this response is rooted in experience. Sociology teaches us to pause, reflect, and interrogate normative understandings of social phenomena. We strive to make the familiar strange. I encourage all of us to take a step back, think about the impact of trust on organizational relationships, and consider whether collective skepticism might be a better position from which organizations should engage.

ACKNOWLEDGMENTS

Neighborhoods are ever-changing, dynamic spaces. The Greater Engle-wood and Little Village of today are not the same places they were when I conducted my fieldwork, and for some residents these neighborhoods have improved; for others they have not. The intention of this book, however, was not to portray these neighborhoods as they are; it was to capture a brief moment that underscores how community members can strategically enact change and claim ownership over their neigh-borhoods. Such a project is, inevitably, a collaborative endeavor, and as a result I owe a huge debt of gratitude to the residents and commu-nity organizers of both Little Village and Greater Englewood. Many of the people I would like to thank will remain anonymous—they are the Chicago residents, activists, scholars, and journalists who trusted me enough to share their experiences with development in the city. I would especially like to thank members of Enlace, the Little Village Envi-ronmental Justice Organization, the Resident Association of Greater Englewood, Sustainable Englewood Initiatives, Teamwork Englewood, and Universidad Popular for their willingness to open their minds, schedules, and organizations to me. Without their consent to allow yet *another* researcher into their midst, this project would not have been possible.

I would especially like to thank the community activists, most of whom are women of color, for keeping me informed about community-led projects, for including me in their campaigns, and for allowing me to spend countless hours hanging out at their community meetings, and talking to residents, volunteers, and staff. I would like to thank members of the Local Initiatives Support Corporation for taking the time to speak with me and for their support of the project. I would also like to thank members of DePaul's Egan Institute; their guidance and insight on the history of the New Communities Project in both Greater Englewood and Little Village and its relationship to broader citywide redevelopment goals were instrumental to my work. In addition, I would like to thank the staff at both the Chicago History Museum's Research Center and the Harold Washington Library Municipal Collection.

This project, and my career as a sociologist, would not have been possible without the training, feedback, and support that I received at the City Colleges of Chicago, Harold Washington campus; at Smith College; and at the University of California, Berkeley. It was during my time at Smith that I first learned about the impact of Latinos/as/xs on the United States. My undergraduate mentor, Dr. Ginetta E. B. Candelario, encouraged me to "use my intellect and channel my anger" regarding social inequities in development toward uncovering hidden truths and social phenomena as they relate to racialized populations. It was during our weekly conversations that I first made connections across development, social networks, and the life chances of those in impoverished communities of color. I am eternally grateful for her support. Extended conversations with Margaret Weir, Claude Fisher, and Martín Sanchez-Jankowski regarding the broader impacts of social policy on communities of color were instrumental to my thinking about development beyond gentrification. Jonathan Wynn's careful eye, witty feedback, and constant support have been integral to the completion of this project.

My colleagues at Knox College—Nancy Eberhardt, Lawrence (Larry) Breitborde, and William Hope—taught me to be a better ethnographer and to "not be boring!" I hope I've lived up to the challenge. Conversations with the phenomenal women at the Five College Women's Studies Research Center, particularly Amy Cox Hall, Jennifer Hamilton, Mary Njeri Kinyanjui, Charlotte Krarlokke, Patricia Montoya, Loretta Ross, Lauren Silber, and Jennifer Zenovich, were instrumental in extending my work in key ways. Hannah Holleman, Caroline Melly, and Ellen Pader inspired me to think through the broader complications of building trust between researchers and informants in ethnography. María Elena Cepeda, Margaret Cerullo, Daniel Egan, Marla Erlien, Angela Fillingim, Manata Hashemi, Sue Kim, and Vanessa Rosa provided feedback on several areas of the manuscript; I am grateful for their support of the project during my many crises of doubt and for reminding me to trust my instincts. Additionally, I am grateful to Karla Medina, who served as my research assistant on this project.

I am grateful to my colleagues at the University of Massachusetts, Lowell, especially in the Department of Sociology and the Pre-Tenure Women of Color Working Group. Joselyne Chenane Nkogo, Yayara Michel, and Angela Walter provided important feedback during presentations of this work. Jannette Marquez kept me organized and ensured that I had access to all of the images that I needed. Debra Osnowitz and Lauren Rubenzahl were integral to fine-tuning the final manuscript. I would also like to thank the anonymous reviewers for their detailed feedback and for pushing me to clarify my ideas. Working with the editorial team at New York University Press has been a joy. I'm grateful to Victor Rios, Pierrette Hondagneu-Sotelo, Sonia Tsuruoka, and, especially, Ilene Kalish for their support of the project.

The time and funds to complete this work would not have been possible without the support of several institutions. I am grateful to the Social Science Research Council—Mellon Mays Graduate Initiatives Program and the Woodrow Wilson Foundation. I have grown tremendously from the many conversations I've had with other Mellon-Mays Fellows and am thankful for the integral space that the SSRC has created for scholars of color.

Finally, I would like to thank my family and friends who supported me throughout this endeavor. Even though they may not have always understood what I was doing, my mother and siblings provided profound support over the years. They offered a couch to crash on during research trips, let me use their car so I could drive to community meetings, and listened to my "sociology talk" whenever we'd hang out—and they only made fun of me after I left the room. My mommy is deserving of extra gratitude; as a single mother with four unruly, delinquent, bad as hell children, she worked hard to instill in us a curiosity for the world around us, a love of learning and exploring, and a deep sense of social justice. I strive to live up to her example. Without the support, kindness, and understanding of Wilson Valentín-Escobar, I would not have had as much fun during this process. Not only did he provide constant reminders about why I should continue my work, he also reminded me to dance. I am indebted to Melissa Nuttelman and Peter Senser. They provided a safe haven to write, interesting conversation, and tremendous support throughout the writing phases. Lastly, I'd like to thank Monika Martinez, Roberto Medina, and Keti Loncar. These three wonderful people kept me grounded, introduced me to key community members in Little Village and Greater Englewood, accompanied me on research adventures with no questions asked, and made sure that I laughed on a regular basis. I am forever indebted to them for their kindness, support, and friendship.

APPENDIX A

Methods

To better understand the ways that community groups engage with local development decisions, I joined six organizations affiliated with the New Communities Program, three in each neighborhood. I participated in parties, arts events, visioning sessions, data analysis, English-language tutoring, community cleanup drives, creation of GIS maps, and economic development brainstorming. I attended many meetings and met with residents and community organizers in parks, homes, churches, restaurants, libraries, and community centers.

Drawing on approaches to research developed by feminist and ethnic studies scholars and community-engaged researchers, I sought to understand the complicated terrain of nonprofits and community development before beginning interviews. I also pursued ways to build reciprocal relationships with my research partners—I had skills that could assist nonprofits and grassroots organizations, and I sought to work "with" rather than for or against the organizations and residents of Greater Englewood and Little Village. I therefore engaged in those communities for a year before I used my observations, fieldnotes, and casual conversations with residents to frame my questions and finalize my interview guide. This time in the field also allowed me to form my own understanding of the New Communities Program and its effects on these communities.

My questions for community organizers and organizational directors centered on organizations' external relationships, the strength of these network linkages, organizations' collaborative projects, and issues of trust. My interviews offered insight into community nonprofits' involvement with the Local Initiatives Support Corporation, their understanding of their relationships with the corporation and the New Communities Program, and the Local Initiatives Support Corporation's relationship to the neighborhood. My interviews with staff from that organization illuminated its views about the importance of its programs and its relation to the community-based nonprofits it serves. Taking an informant-as-expert approach, I sought to understand organizational environments, views of local economic development, relations between community-based nonprofits and the New Communities Program, and problems (if any) that directors of neighborhood nonprofits foresaw in working (or not) with the Local Initiatives Support Corporation.[1] I explored the same questions with corporation staff, allowing these informants to teach me about their views of the problems, questions, and situations regarding the New Communities Program. This open-ended process minimized the potential for me to overlook important aspects of the development process.[2]

In conjunction with my own interview and observational data, I drew from archival documents regarding programming and funding that were housed at the Local Initiatives Support Corporation, community-based organizations, the Metro Chicago Information Center, the Harold Washington Municipal Reference Collection, and the Chicago Historical Museum.[3] To situate the organizational universe within Chicago and New Communities Program neighborhoods, I used data from GuidestStar, the U.S. Census 2000, the American Community Survey 2009, and the New Communities Program. These sources provided information about funding histories, foundation and government funders, local economic development projects, and amounts funneled to low-income neighborhoods through the Local Initiatives Support Corporation. Using publicly available data, I compiled descriptive statistics regarding Chicago, New Communities–affiliated neighborhoods, and funding directed to neighborhood-based nonprofits.

As my analysis proceeded, I presented my work at the Five College Women's Studies Research Center, where colleagues encouraged me to interrogate the ways that trust, mistrust, and collective skepticism operated not only between organizational members but also between my informants and me.[4] This consideration was important. Qualitative research—and ethnography in particular—requires a high level of immersion and relationship building between the researcher and project participants to ensure that the researcher understands the social processes in operation. Scholars have therefore highlighted the importance of building trust as a precondition for uncovering certain "truths." This process, however, primarily serves the researcher and rarely provides much to communities in return.[5] That is, although the researcher may seek assurance that informants are engaging honestly, she ultimately has little to lose in these partnerships.

Indeed, the cultivation of trust may violate a researcher's ethical imperative to do no harm. If a researcher does not clearly articulate the manner of the research project, participants may mistakenly view participation as an indication that some aspect of their lives will change for the better or that they will be presented in a wholly positive manner. If no benefits emerge, participants may develop feelings of disdain, frustration, and deep mistrust of scholarship. For many populations, participation in academic research rarely directly benefits their communities, and for racially and economically marginalized populations that are overstudied, research often adds an extra layer of exploitation. People with whom I have worked in both urban and rural spaces frequently highlight this point. Regardless of our intentions, academic researchers (especially those of us who are pre-tenure) are constrained by our university affiliations, which can limit our capacity for slow, intentional, and transformative work that addresses the social problems we study.

Community organizers in Greater Englewood and Little Village had a deep understanding of these tensions. Seeking to ensure that I presented their work and their organizations accurately and in the best light, groups in both neighborhoods found ways to work with me. Some of the people I worked with checked in from time to time with questions about my research; others asked to read early drafts of my findings. A few asked to have their responses removed. Some youth organizers presented alongside me on academic panels, others invited me to fundraising events, and some asked for advice on or insight into certain issues. Some were cautious in our conversations, but most of my informants wanted their stories told and their work recorded, even as they wanted to influence my presentation. As a result, throughout the book I attempt to balance community groups' narratives with the actions I observed. Nevertheless, these tensions highlight the challenges in attempting to build trust between researchers and community groups.

So does trust have a place in ethnography? Not in the traditional sense. Trust requires a vulnerability that university researchers are unable to extend, and as a result we must always remind our informants that we are researchers first. We can, however, cultivate collective skepticism of our work and its effects. That is, as sociologists we should welcome a questioning environment that forces us to interrogate our research agendas and approaches. Such a process promotes realistic expectations for the research and reinforces the reality that the relationship between researcher and informants is transactional. For those of us who work with marginalized populations, this requires a constant awareness of power differentials between ourselves and informants. Several scholars have successfully developed lasting relationships by sharing their findings with informants and treating community groups as collaborators rather than passive respondents. Researchers need regularly to remind informants of their research agendas, and we need also to remind *ourselves* of our personal and professional intentions.

In-Depth Interview Protocol

Background Information:
1. Can you please describe your organization? (What type of work you do in the community/city? How long has this organization been around?)
2. Are your organization's interests local, state-wide, or national in scope?
3. Can you please describe your role in the organization?
4. How would you define development in your neighborhood? (If necessary, give examples.)
5. What development projects has your organization worked on in the past? And currently?

Networks and Development:
6. Is there an organization that makes the major decisions in your neighborhood?
7. If a project were before the community and required a decision by a group of leaders/organizations, how many decision holders actually need to be present to get the project moving? Do any of the above-mentioned organizations/leaders need to be present?
8. Can you give me an example of a recent project where several organizations came together in order to plan it and implement it?
   a. Have you worked with these organizations on other projects since the initial project? Can you tell me a little about that?
9. Are there other city-wide or neighborhood-wide organizations that you can depend on when it comes to neighborhood-based projects? Can you tell which ones those are?

10. How often do you initiate an interaction with these organizations? What types of resources do you receive from your relationship with these organizations? (For instance, advice, funds, friendship and social enjoyment, information on organizational guidance and opportunities, etc.?)
11. Are there one or two organizations that you tend to initiate contact with more often? (If yes) Can you describe that relationship? (If no) Can you explain why not?

Attitudes and Opinions on Coalition Building:
12. What do you think are the positive aspects of collaborating on projects and/or coalition building?
13. What do you think are the negative aspects of collaborating on projects and/or coalition building?
14. What do you think about coalition building in your community?
15. Do you think this is different from other (Black/Latina/o) neighborhoods? Why/Why not?

Coalition Building/Collaboration Networks:
16. Do you belong to any organizational coalitions? What organizations make up those coalitions?
17. Have you ever approached anyone about building a coalition?
    a. (If yes) Can you tell me about it?
        i. Who do you ask, and why do you ask that person/organization?
        ii. What type of organization is it?
        iii. Would you say that this organization or person has power or influence in the neighborhood?
        iv. Has this person/organization helped you on more than one occasion?
        v. How did this person/organization help?
        vi. Did you collaborate on any projects with this organization? Or did the organization introduce you/include you on any coalitions?
    b. (If no) Is there any reason why you haven't reached out to others to collaborate?

18. Has anyone ever come to you in order to collaborate on a project?
    a. Who has come and why?
    b. What types of projects did this person or organization want to collaborate on?
    c. Did you collaborate with the person(s) or organization? Or introduce them to a coalition?
    d. Can you describe your role in the collaboration?
    e. Would you collaborate again? (If yes) Why? (If no) Why not?
19. When people approach you to collaborate on projects or to form coalitions, how do you determine if you will help them or not?

Who Knows Whom and Who Wants to Work with Whom:
20. Are there any organizations in the community that you would like to work with? Why?
21. Are there any city-wide organizations that you would like to work with? Why?

Trust:
22. One of the things that has come up in terms of a challenge to coalition building and development has been trust or mistrust of other organizations. Do you agree that this is a challenge? Can you explain your answer? What do you think can lead to more trust in development?

NOTES

INTRODUCTION

Epigraphs: Morrison (2003), Anzaldúa (1987, 3).

1 During my adolescence and beyond, people of Mexican descent in Chicago referred to themselves as Mexican or Mexican American. The term "Chicana/o/x" is not prevalent except among some of the college educated.

2 Despite a growing population of Afro-Latinas/os/xs throughout Chicago, most of the Black population is African American. I use Black and African American interchangeably throughout.

3 Rios (2015).

4 For a discussion of Latina/o/x usage, see Pelaez Lopez (2018), Trujillo-Pagán (2018), and Guidotti-Hernández (2017).

5 Pilsen was included as one of the sixteen neighborhoods in the New Communities Program.

6 According to a report compiled by DePaul University, developers are particularly attracted to Pilsen because most of the land is zoned for three-flat townhomes (RT-4), yet many of the homes on these lots are single-story (Curran and Hague 2006). This mismatch in zoning means that a developer can buy a single-story, RT-4-zoned home, demolish it, and then rebuild a larger three-flat condominium without having to petition the zoning board for a change.

7 Fainstein (2011).

8 Malizia and Feser (1999) and Wolman and Spitzley (1996), for example.

9 Lees, Bang Shin, and López-Morales (2016), Lees, Wyly, and Slater (2008), Wacquant (2008), Smith (1996).

10 Researchers have found both positive and negative effects of gentrification. It can increase amenities within a neighborhood and social capital for residents but can also lead to displacement and loss of social networks (decreasing social capital), increase social isolation, and exacerbate the effects of poverty.

11 Wacquant (2008), Smith and Williams (1986).

12 Rodriguez (2014), Vargas (2014), Bonds (2013), McQuarrie (2010), Taylor and Puente (2004), Smith (1996).

13 Sometimes also referred to as community economic development or community development.

14 Green and Haines (2012), Emejulu (2011), Greenwood and Holt (2010), Simon (2001).

15 Rios and Vazquez (2012).

16 As defined by the Environmental Protection Agency, brownfield sites are places that contain potentially hazardous substances, pollutants, or contaminants.

17 McQuarrie (2013), Lowe (2008), Kumar and Corbridge (2002).

18 McQuarrie (2013), Silverman (2005), Rusk (1999), Weir (1999), Temkin and Rohe (1998), Stoecker (1997), Salamon (1995).

19 Fainstein (2011).

20 Fainstein (2011), McQuarrie (2010), Marwell (2007), Simon (2001).

21 Marwell (2007).

22 Marwell (2007), Ferguson and Stoutland (1999).

23 Stoutland (1999).

24 Weir (1999).

25 McQuarrie (2013).

26 Salamon (1995).

27 Pastor, Benner, and Matsuoka (2009).

28 Hirsch (2005).

29 This includes the retirement of Chicago's longtime mayor Richard M. Daley, who served for twenty-two years, and the subsequent elections of President Obama's former chief of staff, Mayor Rahm Emanuel, and Chicago's first Black woman mayor, Lori Lightfoot.

30 The MacArthur Foundation is a private Chicago-based foundation that, among its other national and international endeavors, supports local initiatives within Chicago. MacArthur granted $50 million to the Local Initiatives Support Corporation for the initiative. The $900 million reflects the grants that streamed into the neighborhoods as a result of the New Communities Program.

31 Founded in 1978 in the South Bronx, Banana Kelly provides a variety of safety-net programming to local residents. The organization primarily focuses on increasing and retaining affordable housing units in New York City.

32 To better streamline and coordinate community development initiatives, the Ford Foundation set aside $10 million to fund the Local Initiatives Support Corporation. Clemens and Guthrie (2010).

33 These numbers reflect growth from eighteen cities and five states in 2014.

34 Pastor, Benner, and Matsuoka (2009), Lowe (2008).

35 Rankin (2015), Walker, Rankin, and Winston (2010).

36 Since President Johnson's War on Poverty, urban policies across the nation have attempted to address ongoing issues of concentrated poverty. Examples of programs include Model Cities, Special Impact Program, Community Action, CDBG grants, empowerment zones, enterprise zones, and tax increment financing districts.

37 O'Connor (1999).

38 O'Connor (1999), Weir (1999).

39 Weir (1999).

40 O'Connor (1999).

41 McQuarrie (2013), Fainstein (2011), Wacquant (2008), Boger and Wegner (1996), Smith (1996), Logan and Molotch (1987), Smith and Williams (1986).

42 Vargas (2016).

43 Garrison (2007).

44 Angotti (2012), Dávila (2004).

45 Wherry (2011, 3).

46 Elsewhere I discuss the ways that race and class intersect with community work in Chicago. "Ratchet-Rasquache Activism: Aesthetic and Discursive Frames within Chicago-Based Women-of-Color Activism," *Social Problems*, was published in 2020, and "Semillas de Justicia: Chicana Environmentalism in Chicago" will appear in *Latinas and the Politics of Urban Spaces*, edited by Sharon Navarro and Lillian A. Saldaña.

47 Vargas (2016), Marwell (2007).

48 See, for example, Lara (2018), DelSesto (2015), McQuarrie (2013), Clemens and Guthrie (2010), Ferguson and Stoutland (1999), Keyes et al. (1996).

CHAPTER 1. *ÀSE*

Epigraph: Destina Kunze, interview by Teresa Gonzales, September 2016. Note: All individuals' names are pseudonyms, except when quoting from newspaper articles or public comments made by local politicians.

1 Small (2009), Smith (2007), Massey (1996), Putnam (1995), and Wilson (1987), to name a few.

2 Chua, Ingram, and Morris (2008, 436); Rousseau et al. (1998, 395).

3 Zolin and Hinds (2004), Kroeger (2011).

4 Zielenbach (2000), Fukuyama (1995), Putnam (1994).

5 For this study, grassroots groups refer to residents of a community who come together to solve a neighborhood-based issue. This includes formal and nonformal organizations, such as nonprofits, community-based organizations, resident associations, and block clubs. Tsasis (2009), Smith (2007), Small (2004, 2009), Keyes et al. (1996).

6 Lambright, Mischen, and Laramee (2010), Tsasis (2009), Putnam (1995).

7 Sander and Putnam (2010), Small (2009), Smith (2007).

8 Portes and Sensenbrenner (1993).

9 Small (2009), Smith (2007), Coleman (1988), Rotter (1980). See also Chua, Ingram, and Morris (2008).

10 See Dekker and Uslaner (2003) and Putnam (1995).

11 Putnam (1995), Portes and Sensenbrenner (1993).

12 DeFilippis (2001).

13 Ross, Mirowsky, and Pribesh (2001), Massey (1996), Wilson (1987).

14 Smith (2007).

15 Bell (2016).

16 Small (2009).

17 For a discussion of trust, mistrust, and poverty, see, for example, Duncan (2014), Small (2004), Rankin and Quane (2000), and Wilson (1987).

18 Voutira and Harrell-Bond (1995).

19 MSNBC segment, August 13, 2018.

20 Warren (1999), Coleman (1974).

21 Mansuri and Rao (2004), DeFilippis (2001), Hardy, Phillips, and Lawrence (1998).

22 Kroeger (2011), Powell (2007), Hardy, Phillips, and Lawrence (1998), DiMaggio and Powell (1991).

23 Vargas (2016), Marwell (2007).

24 Greenwood and Hinings (2006, 820), Granovetter (1983).

25 Greenwood and Hinings (2006), Scott (2000).

26 Greenwood and Hinings (2006).

27 Fligstein (2001).

28 Merton (1973).

29 Mansbridge (1996).

30 Small (2013), Granovetter (1973, 1983).

31 For the Local Initiatives Support Corporation, vulnerable neighborhoods are areas without access to social services, with the risk of gentrification and/or with prior disinvestment or population change. LISC/Chicago (2011).

32 As of 2019, only partial census-tract-level data on these neighborhoods are available after the 2009 American Community Survey. Given the impact of the Great Recession on Chicago, it is difficult to ascertain direct New Communities Program benefits without using census tract data. Zip-code-level data are not accurate for these communities as those data encompass several neighborhoods. Within Chicago, vacancy rates, education levels, and racial makeup vary dramatically from block to block.

33 Briggs (2002), Kubisch et al. (2002), Chaskin et al. (2001), Kingsley, McNeely, and Gibson (1997), Kubisch et al. (1997).

34 McQuarrie (2010), Marwell (2004, 2007), Weir (1999), Salamon (1987), to name a few.

35 Kretzmann and McKnight (1997, 6).

36 Green and Haines (2012).

37 McQuarrie (2013), Marwell (2007).

38 See Kretzmann and McKnight (1997) and Alinsky (1946).

39 In 2010, the population of Chicago was 2,695,598. Of that, 33 percent identified as African American, 29 percent as Latina/o, and 32 percent as non-Hispanic White. Of the population, 15 percent had less than a high school education. The median income was $47,300, and the unemployment rate was 9 percent, with 21 percent of the population living below the poverty line.

40 A 2014 report by Rob Paral and Associates and the Illinois Coalition for Immigrant and Refugee Rights estimates that Little Village contains a population of 20,000 undocumented immigrants (Tsao 2014).

41 MetroPulse (2017), EPA (2014, 2011, 2008b), Rezin (2013), LVEJO (2009).

42 CNT (2014), Hilkevitch (2014), Jiao and Dillivan (2013).

43 Although the New Communities Program exists only in Englewood, I focus on Greater Englewood because community organizations target both areas when creating programming and residents view the area as one neighborhood.

44 Moser (2011), Olivo, Mullen, and Glanton (2011).

45 See GHN (2014, 12).

46 Zielenbach (2000).

47 Sampson (2012), De Genova (2005), Perez (2004), Zielenbach (2000).

48 The state of Illinois requires that ward boundaries be redrawn after each federal census to ensure equal representation based on population (Knox 2005).

49 Grossman (2013), Keefe (2013).

50 Within Chicago, a community's political strength often comes from both voting rates and ward boundaries. Given the resident-involved planning that went into the New Communities Program's quality-of-life plans, this political strength is important for understanding aldermanic and mayoral support for community-led neighborhood redevelopment projects.

51 Small (2015), Rios (2011), Hoang (2015).

52 Du Bois (1903).

53 Trainor and Bouchard (2012), Huisman (2008).

54 Fraser (1990), Mansbridge (1990).

CHAPTER 2. A SEAT AT THE TABLE

Epigraphs: Comment made by an executive director of a New Communities Program lead agency at a public land use development meeting held on January 28, 2012, in the Washington Park neighborhood of Chicago; Querida Villanueva, interview by Teresa Gonzales, April 19, 2013; Quad Communities organizer, interview by Karla Medina, March 2017.

1 The Local Initiatives Support Corporation is a national community development intermediary.

2 Community-based organizations are formal nonprofit organizations tied to specific geographic regions, such as neighborhoods (Marwell 2007). For a comprehensive discussion of community-based organizations, see Marwell (2007), Ferguson and Stoutland (1999), and Stoutland (1999).

3 For a discussion on how established organizations are able to "bend with the wind" and adapt to changing political, social movement, and funding environments, see Minkoff (1999).

4 Dávila (2004).

5 McQuarrie (2013, 2010), Marwell (2004, 2007), Weir (1999), Salamon (1987).

6 For a discussion on the importance of organizational fields in understanding how local nonprofits operate within urban governance structures, see Marwell (2007).

7 Minkoff (1999), Pfeffer and Salancik ([1978] 2003).

8 Jenkins (1985).

9 In the early 2000s, however, most projects in Chicago did not incorporate resident feedback.

10 Leavitt (2006), Chaskin et al. (2001), Bratt (1997), Porter (1995).

11 As defined by Molotch (1976), growth machines are collective groups of otherwise pluralistic political and economic elites who come together in order to steer urban growth.

12 See Logan and Molotch (1987).

13 Chaskin and Karlström (2012), Finkel (2012), Greenberg et al. (2010).

14 For an overview of visioning, see Shipley (2000).

15 Teamwork Englewood and LISC/Chicago (2005).

16 Enlace and LISC/Chicago (2005).

17 Zielenbach (2000).

18 Greenberg et al. (2010), Bratt and Rohe (2005), Simon (2001).

19 See also Chaskin and Karlström (2012) and Greenberg et al. (2010).

20 Information based on interviews with a Local Initiatives Support Corporation executive director and program officers from the two lead agencies in Englewood and Little Village.

21 These nonprofit staff members may have trusted me enough to discuss their thoughts on redevelopment and the New Communities Program, yet I clearly sensed tension when I passed by these same individuals in the Local Initiatives Support Corporation office. This encounter came up in later conversations with two of them, who were both nervous that I might reveal sensitive information but also curious about the Local Initiatives Support Corporation staff's views of the New Communities Program in their neighborhoods. During all of these conversations, I took care not to divulge personal comments, names, or opinions. Although it was difficult to maintain, the anonymity of my respondents and the confidentiality of their accounts are ethically important.

22 Steven Santos, casual conversation during an event, fieldnotes, October 2011.

23 Faith Brown and Meredith Roe, interview by Teresa Gonzales, 2013.

24 Chaskin and Karlström (2012, 42).

25 Chaskin and Karlström (2012, 37).

26 Marwell (2007), Weir (1999).

27 Chaskin and Karlström (2012, 23–24).

28 Chaskin and Karlström (2012), confirmed by Nereyda Smith during our conversation on March 21, 2013.

29 Chaskin and Karlström (2012, 65).

30 Prior to involvement with the New Communities Program, SWOP was already deeply involved in advocacy. It also had strong preexisting ties to allies in the state legislature and other Chicago-based advocacy organizations. As Minkoff (1999) highlights, the presence of political allies helps to shape the kinds of social movement activity of organizations. Although the New Communities Program increased environmental and organizational constraints on many of their partners, they were unable to influence SWOP's activities in the same way.

31 McQuarrie (2010), Marwell (2004).

32 Marwell (2007), Gittell and Thomson (2001).

33 This connection is discussed further in chapter 4.

34 Chuy for Congress (2014).

35 The data, information from the organizations' 2011 Form 990, were taken from GuideStar.

36 Interviews with the Local Initiatives Support Corporation and Teamwork Englewood program officers.

37 LISC/Chicago (2011).

38 Eric James, interview by Teresa Gonzales, February 20, 2013.

39 Zachary Evans, interview by Teresa Gonzales, October 19, 2012.

40 Chua, Ingram, and Morris (2008), McAllister (1995), O'Reilly (1982).

41 In 2012, the Local Initiatives Support Corporation, with an eight-million-dollar grant from the MacArthur Foundation (MacFound 2012), implemented a follow-up initiative to the New Communities Program whereby organizational members worked with a select few lead agencies in their target neighborhoods. Titled Testing the Model, the initiative aimed to promote data collection as a useful tool for improving upon project goals and tracking accomplishments and future goals. According to the University of Chicago's Chapin Hall, a local policy research center, Testing the Model trains community agencies and "refine[s] the approaches the CBOs are undertaking to address issues in their communities, and to develop tools, processes, and systems for data analysis and performance management" (Rich 2013). As part of this project, Chapin Hall created a centralized data management system that is open to all participating CBOs. In addition, the center provided consultation to the selected lead agencies on educational issues; ways to collect, record, and track performance and outcomes over time; and ways to analyze the collected data (Rich 2013; Kelleher 2012).

CHAPTER 3. "YOU CAN'T DO IT IF YOU'RE MAD, YOU CAN DO IT IF YOU'RE ORGANIZED"

Epigraph: Ernie Jones, interview by Teresa Gonzales, May 28, 2014.

1 This anger and mistrust were articulated at a number of local community meetings, such as at a summit on the state of Englewood held at the downtown location of a local university. Speakers included members of several Englewood-based organizations, including Teamwork Englewood, Illinois state senator Mattie Hunter, and local researchers who study the adverse effects of poverty on health. In order to ensure "community representation," approximately fifty residents of Greater Englewood were bussed into the downtown area for the summit. During the question-and-answer period, several residents stood up and voiced their frustration with Teamwork Englewood, other local nonprofits, and local political representation. One resident in particular noted that many nonprofits make a lot of money off of the poor in Englewood via social services, but nobody—not the organizations, not the city, not the local politicians—works to actually eradicate

the conditions of poverty within his and other Black communities. This resident went on to further highlight the disconnect between local nonprofits and community members in Greater Englewood. For this resident, the location of the summit was a prime example of this fissure: rather than hosting the summit in the heart of Greater Englewood and ensure a larger, possibly more critical, audience, organizers chose to hold the meeting in downtown Chicago. This frustration with the local nonprofit field in Greater Englewood was exhibited at several community meetings across the neighborhood and city.

2 For instance, see Gonzales (2017), Pastor, Benner, and Matsuoka (2009), Zielenbach (2000), Squires et al. (1987), Wilson (1987).

3 Pyles (2014).

4 Pyles (2014), Barker, Johnson, and Lavalette (2001), Pharr (1996), Alinsky (1971).

5 See Worthy et al. (2016).

6 See Pastor, Benner, and Matsuoka (2009, 15).

7 Benit-Gbaffou and Katsaura (2014), Stone et al. (1999), Stoutland (1999), Gilchrist and Taylor (1997), Hart, Jones, and Bains (1997).

8 Polletta (2002), Barker, Johnson, and Lavalette (2001), Burns (1978).

9 Polletta (2002), Melucci (1996), Burns (1978).

10 Haus and Sweeting (2006), Polletta (2002), Barker, Johnson, and Lavalette (2001), Burns (1978).

11 Benit-Gbaffou and Katsaura (2014), Chen and Graddy (2010), Small (2009), Polletta (2002), Barker, Johnson, and Lavalette (2001), Bockmeyer (2000), Gregory (1999), Burns (1978).

12 This relationship developed partly because of the Local Initiatives Support Corporation's former executive director, who was previously a board member, executive director at the Chicago Housing Authority, and coauthor of Chicago's Plan for Transformation. This person left the Local Initiatives Support Corporation to head Chicago's Department of Housing and Economic Development in 2010.

13 Comprehensive neighborhood quality-of-life plans are discussed in chapter 2.

14 Research on community activism by women of color highlights the importance of autonomy. See Isoke (2013), Seyfang and Longhurst (2013), Grimshaw (2011), Collins (2000), and Rodriguez (1998).

15 This summit was held to expand the environmental justice movement to include issues raised by communities of color across the globe. The summit bolstered the environmental justice movement to include broader issues of public health, land use, transportation, housing, community empowerment, and worker rights (Connell 2011).

16 The data, information from the organizations' 2011 Form 990, were taken from GuideStar.

17 The interns were from DePaul University, the Illinois Institute of Art, the School of the Art Institute of Chicago, the University of Illinois at Chicago, and the University of Illinois at Urbana-Champaign.

18 Located on Chicago's Southeast Side and currently one of the most diverse communities in the city, Bridgeport is historically a working-class White neighborhood. Five of Chicago's mayors, including Richard J. Daley and Richard M. Daley, either were born or lived in Bridgeport.

19 Chicago's Museum Campus is a park that surrounds three museums as well as a football stadium and conference center.

20 Anonymous, fieldnotes, 2012.

21 The meeting took place on August 8, 2012, at CTA's headquarters.

22 As part of R.A.G.E.'s inclusive stance, the organization included a small percentage of White, Asian, and Latina/o/x members.

23 In 2017, Asiaha Butler quit her job to focus on R.A.G.E.'s mission full-time.

24 With the exception of the Greater Englewood and Back of the Yards neighborhoods, most communities fall almost completely in one or two wards. Little Village is spread across three wards; however, the majority of the community is within the Twenty-Second Ward.

25 Gibbs (2015).

26 The deaths in Afghanistan and Iraq came as part of Operation Enduring Freedom and Operation Iraqi Freedom.

27 Suppelsa (2013).

28 Anonymous, fieldnotes, 2011.

29 These quotes are based on a conversation with R.A.G.E. members at a community meeting in April 2012.

30 The goal of the Chicago Alternative Policing Strategy (CAPS), implemented in 1994 across Chicago, was to blend traditional policing with alternative strategies and thus to encourage police and residents to work together and reduce crime rates. CAPS emphasizes increased communication between police and community residents.

31 Ernie Jones, interview by Teresa Gonzales, March 26, 2012.

32 Christian Jimenez, interview by Teresa Gonzales, March 30, 2012.

33 Cathy Jean, interview by Teresa Gonzales, October 16, 2012.

34 Giloth et al. (1992), Vidal (1992), Clay (1990), Mayer and Blake (1984).

35 Fainstein (2011), Polletta (2002).

CHAPTER 4. "TEAMWORK TO MAKE THE DREAM WORK"

Epigraph: Nikki Song, interview by Karla Medina, March 2017.

1 Popular in Aguada, Puerto Rico, and Chicago, the *jibarito* is a deliciously salty sandwich made with flattened, fried green plantains instead of bread, steak, garlic mayonnaise, cheese, tomato, and lettuce.

2 Anonymous, fieldnotes, 2011.

3 Collective efficacy represents the combined effects of social cohesion, through ties, networks, and shared goals, among neighbors and a willingness to intervene on behalf of the common good.

4 See Sampson (2012) and Fung (2004).

5 Ennis and West (2012), Sánchez-Jankowski (2008), Smith (2007), Pfeffer and Salancik ([1978] 2003), Cross et al. (2001), Sampson and Raudenbush (1999), Weir (1999), Davis and Greve (1997), Keyes et al. (1996), Putnam (1994, 1995).

6 CMAP (2012, 27).

7 Authorized under Title III of the Housing and Economic Recovery Act of 2008, HUD's neighborhood stabilization program provides federal funds to state and local governments and other organizations so that they can acquire and redevelop foreclosed properties that might become sources of blight and abandonment. These grants can be used to rehabilitate, resell, or redevelop homes in order to stabilize the housing stock and housing values of a neighborhood.

8 McCarron (2011).

9 The Chicago Plan Commission approved the plan on March 20, 2014. Established in 1909, the commission reviews land use proposals, planned developments, planned manufacturing districts, industrial corridors, tax increment financing districts, community land use plans, and the sale and acquisition of public land.

10 The farm sells their produce on site at cost and accepts a variety of publicly funded food payment plans (SNAP, EBT, LINK, WIC). Furthermore, residents who use any of these payment options receive double benefits up to twenty dollars (i.e., twenty dollars' worth of produce for ten dollars).

11 Spielman (2013b).

12 Tax increment financing (TIF) is a public financing method that is used to subsidize redevelopment, infrastructure improvements, and/or other community improvement projects. Adopted in Illinois in 1977, the Tax Increment Allocation Redevelopment Act (TIF Act) allows municipal governments to redirect property taxes to fund economic redevelopment initiatives in blighted or declining areas. According to data compiled by the Chicago-based Civic Lab and the Cook County Clerk's Office, the City of Chicago reallocated approximately five billion dollars in property taxes between 1986 and 2011. Critics of TIFs in Chicago indicate the mayor's ability to use these funds without oversight. A study by the Better Government Association highlighted Mayor Rahm Emanuel's use of TIF funds to expand the downtown tourist attraction Navy Pier.

13 Greenwood and Holt (2010), Simon (2001).

14 Greenwood and Holt (2010), Sánchez-Jankowski (2008).

15 Small (2009), Sánchez-Jankowski (2008), Portes and Stepick (1993), Aldrich and Waldinger (1990).

16 Gonzales (2017), Sampson (2012).

17 According to the website of the Chicago Department of Planning and Development, "The Adjacent Neighbors Land Acquisition Program allows homeowners in certain areas within the city of Chicago to purchase vacant city-owned lots for less than market value if the parcel meets certain criteria." Through this program, homeowners were able to purchase an abandoned city-owned lot directly adjacent to their own property for a fraction of the market price. Many homeowners made

such purchases to expand their yard, build a garage, or enlarge their existent home.

18 CMAP and HED (2013).

19 To address the presence of abandoned and vacant properties, the City of Chicago instituted a number of land use initiatives: the Preserving Communities Together Program (PCT), Troubled Building Initiative (TBI), Adjacent Neighbors Land Acquisition Program, and Large Lot Program. PCT encouraged applicants to identify potential non-government-owned abandoned or vacant properties for city acquisition. These sites were sold to developers at a fraction of their market value, with the expectation that, once developed and rehabbed, these sites would be resold to an income-qualified owner-occupant. TBI operated to "compel landlords to maintain safe and drug-free environments." Under Mayor Rahm Emanuel, PCT and TBI were combined into a single initiative.

20 Sfondeles (2014).

21 The grants included $100 million from Transportation Investment Generating Economic Recovery (TIGER) funds, $10.4 million from TIGER IV, $133 million from the American Recovery and Reinvestment Act, $1.25 million from the Federal Railroad Administration, $132 million from Infrastructure for Rebuilding America, and $49.9 million from the Illinois Department of Transportation Competitive Freight Program Application.

22 Information based on the author's attendance at these public meetings and interviews conducted with Yvonne Daniels and Fae Jenkins from the Illinois Department of Transportation.

23 CREATE includes seventy projects, eight of which affect the Greater Englewood community.

24 Chicago Mayor's Press Office (2013), SEI (2013).

25 Spielman (2013a).

26 The 104 parcels sold for $1,105,000 and were located near the boundaries of Garfield Boulevard, Wallace Street, Stewart Avenue, and West Sixty-First Street.

27 Olivo (2006). A 1995 federal law states that the Surface Transportation Board is responsible for the regulation of rail operations.

28 CSX agreed to pay $300,000 a year for twenty years (1998–2018) into the fund; the agency has also hosted local parades and contributed $2,000 toward a community center.

29 A video of part of the hearing can be found here: https://youtu.be/kYgseqFbSd4.

30 SEI (2013), Spielman (2013a).

31 LVCDC (2005, 4).

32 Mitchell (2011).

33 In November 2006, the New Communities Program (NCP) unveiled an investment portfolio that consisted of fourteen "investment-ready" opportunities for the City of Chicago (NCP 2006, 5). Included was the Little Village Park Campaign, which called for the creation of a park at the site of the former Washburne Trade School at 3100 South Kedzie Avenue (NCP 2005). The report outlined an

investment opportunity of $5 million for demolition and an overall project value of $25 million.

34 The Little Village Park Campaign portfolio indicated the Chicago Department of Planning and Development, the Chicago Park District, Chicago Public Schools, and Little Village community members as partners on the project.

35 Chaskin and Karlström (2012).

36 Discussion with the executive director of a Little Village nonprofit.

37 Mario Rivera, interview by Teresa Gonzales, October 22, 2012.

38 EPA (2008a).

39 The pollutants were polyaromatic hydrocarbons.

40 Pellow (2002), Hunter (2000), Maher (1998), Anderton et al. (1994).

41 Tessum et al. (2019), Taylor (2014), Maher (1998).

42 LVEJO (2009).

43 Charrettes are meetings where all stakeholders in a project attempt to resolve conflicts and create solutions.

44 *Pan dulce* is Mexican sweet bread.

45 Slife (2010).

46 Little Village Land (2010).

47 In 2011, the city purchased the twenty-four-acre parcel for $7.5 million, and $16 million was committed for the park: $4 million from the City of Chicago, $4 million from the Park District, and $8 million from the State of Illinois (Acevedo 2011).

48 For a discussion on mutual dependence, see Casciaro and Piskorski (2005).

CONCLUSION

Epigraphs: Naila Sanchez, interview by Teresa Gonzales, April 2014; Ernie Jones, interview by Teresa Gonzales, March 26, 2012.

1 Greenberg et al. (2010), Minkoff (1999).

2 Within the United States, place-based policies, focused on a defined geographic space, tend to target economically depressed areas, such as deteriorated downtowns and business corridors in both small towns and large cities experiencing deindustrialization. Examples of place-based policies include empowerment zones, enterprise zones, and tax increment financing districts. As part of the Empowerment Zones Program, both empowerment and enterprise zones use public funds to attract businesses that will create jobs in economically distressed areas. Tax increment financing districts use a portion of local property taxes to subsidize redevelopment, infrastructure improvements, or other community improvement projects within a specific geographic region, such as a neighborhood.

3 Emejulu (2011, 386).

4 Lara (2018).

5 Bonilla-Silva and Baiocchi (2008), Skocpol (2003).

6 Fainstein (2011), Skocpol (2003).

7 Greenwood and Holt (2010), Simon (2001).

8 McQuarrie (2013), Greenwood and Holt (2010), Silverman (2005), Simon (2001).
9 McQuarrie (2013), Silverman (2005).
10 Benit-Gbaffou and Katsaura (2014), Chen and Graddy (2010), Polletta (2002), Barker, Johnson, and Lavalette (2001), Bockmeyer (2000), Taylor (2000), Gregory (1999), Burns (1978).

APPENDIX A

1 Dexter (2006).
2 Both my interview schedule and a breakdown of my data can be found in Appendix B.
3 Founded in 1990, the Metro Chicago Information Center (MCIC) collected demographic information for the six-county metropolitan Chicago area. With a specialization in difficult-to-reach and underserved populations, the MCIC provided data to various research, nonprofit, philanthropic, and governmental agencies across the region. Because of budgetary constraints, the MCIC closed in 2012.
4 The Five College Women's Studies Research Center is housed at Mount Holyoke College in South Hadley, Massachusetts.
5 For a detailed discussion of the ways that ethnographers replicate and reify power inequities, see Small (2015).

BIBLIOGRAPHY

INTERVIEWS

Adams, Virginia. Fieldnotes, September 2012.

Alarcón, Lucia. Interview by Teresa Gonzales, October 19, 2011.

Anonymous. Fieldnotes, 2011.

Anonymous. Fieldnotes, 2012.

Baez, Willy. Interview by Teresa Gonzales, November 2016.

Brown, Faith, and Meredith Roe. Interview by Teresa Gonzales, 2013.

Cadiz, Yazmin. Interview by Teresa Gonzales, October 19, 2012.

Charles, Xavia. Interview by Teresa Gonzales, September 21, 2012.

Czelusniak, Xenia. Interview by Teresa Gonzales, August 2016.

Davis, Yves. Interview by Teresa Gonzales, October 25, 2012.

Evans, Zachary. Interview by Teresa Gonzales, October 19, 2012.

Executive director of a CDC. Interview by Teresa Gonzales, July 22, 2008.

Gomez, Diana. Interview by Teresa Gonzales, October 3, 2012.

Hampton, Douglas. Fieldnotes, 2016.

James, Eric. Interview by Teresa Gonzales, February 20, 2013.

Jaspar, Christine, and Jordan Ng. Interview by Teresa Gonzales, July 2016.

Jean, Cathy. Interview by Teresa Gonzales, October 16, 2012.

Jimenez, Christian. Interview by Teresa Gonzales, March 30, 2012.

Jones, Ernie. Interview by Teresa Gonzales, March 26, 2012.

Jones, Ernie. Interview by Teresa Gonzales, May 28, 2014.

Kunze, Destina. Interview by Teresa Gonzales, September 2016.

LISC. Interview by Teresa Gonzales, 2011.

Montoya, Nancy. Interview by Teresa Gonzales, December 4, 2012.

Muñoz, Hilary. Interview by Teresa Gonzales, November 19, 2012.

Quad Communities organizer. Interview by Karla Medina, March 2017.

Rivera, Mario. Interview by Teresa Gonzales, October 22, 2012.

Rodriguez, Marta. Interview by Teresa Gonzales, October 19, 2012.

Rojas, Diego. Interview by Teresa Gonzales, October 22, 2012.

Sanchez, Naila. Interview by Teresa Gonzales, April 2014.

Santos, Steven. Fieldnotes, October 2011.

Smith, Nereyda, and Betsy West. Interview by Teresa Gonzales, March 21, 2013.

Song, Nikki. Interview by Karla Medina, March 2017.

Villanueva, Querida. Interview by Teresa Gonzales, April 19, 2013.

SECONDARY SOURCES

Acevedo, Carlos. 2011. "Little Village to Receive Long Awaited Park." *Lawndale News*, October 20. www.lawndalenews.com.

Aldrich, Howard E., and Roger Waldinger. 1990. "Ethnicity and Entrepreneurship." *Annual Review of Sociology* 16:111–35.

Alinsky, Saul. 1946. *Reveille for Radicals*. Chicago: University of Chicago Press.

——. 1971. *Rules for Radicals: A Practical Primer for Realistic Radicals*. New York: Random House.

Anderton, Douglas L., Andy B. Anderson, John Michael Oakes, and Michael R. Fraser. 1994. "Environmental Equity: The Demographics of Dumping." *Demography* 31(2):229–48.

Angotti, Tom. 2012. "Placemaking in New York City: From Puerto Rican to Pan-Latino." In *Diálogos: Placemaking in Latino Communities*, edited by Michael Rios, Leonardo Vazquez, and Lucrezia Miranda. New York: Routledge.

Anzaldúa, Gloria. 1987. *Borderlands / La Frontera: The New Mestiza*. San Francisco: Aunt Lute Books.

Barker, Colin, Alan Johnson, and Michael Lavalette, eds. 2001. *Leadership and Social Movements*. Manchester: Manchester University Press.

Bell, Monica. 2016. "Situational Trust: How Disadvantaged Mothers Reconceive Legal Cynicism." *Law & Society Review* 50(2):314–47.

Benit-Gbaffou, Claire, and Obvious Katsaura. 2014. "Community Leadership and the Construction of Political Legitimacy: Unpacking Bourdieu's 'Political Capital' in Post-Apartheid Johannesburg." *International Journal of Urban and Regional Research* 38(5):1807–32.

Bockmeyer, J. L. 2000. "A Culture of Distrust: The Impact of Local Political Culture on Participation in the Detroit EZ." *Urban Studies* 37(13):2417–40.

Boger, John Charles, and Judith Welch Wegner, eds. 1996. *Race Poverty and American Cities*. Chapel Hill: University of North Carolina Press.

Bonds, Anne. 2013. "Economic Development, Racialization, and Privilege: 'Yes in My Backyard' Prison Politics and the Reinvention of Madras, Oregon." *Annals of the Association of American Geographers* 103(6):1389–1405.

Bonilla-Silva, Eduardo, and Gianpaolo Baiocchi. 2008. "Anything but Racism: How Sociologists Limit the Significance of Racism." In *White Logic, White Methods: Racism and Methodology*, edited by Eduardo Bonilla-Silva and Tukufu Zuberi. Lanham, MD: Rowman & Littlefield.

Bratt, Rachel G. 1997. "CDCs: Contributions Outweigh Contradictions, a Reply to Randy Stoecker." *Journal of Urban Affairs* 19(1):23–28.

Bratt, Rachel G., and William Rohe. 2005. "Challenges and Dilemmas Facing Community Development Corporations in the United States." *Community Development Journal* 42(1):63–78.

Briggs, Xavier de Souza. 2002. *The Will and the Way: Local Partnerships, Political Strategy, and the Well-Being of America's Children and Youth*. Cambridge, MA: Harvard University Press.

Burns, James MacGregor. 1978. *Leadership*. New York: Harper & Row.

Casciaro, Tiziana, and Mikolaj Jan Piskorski. 2005. "Power Imbalance, Mutual Dependence, and Constraint Absorption: A Closer Look at Resource Dependence Theory." *Administrative Science Quarterly* 50:167–99.

Chaskin, Robert J., Prudence Brown, Sudhir Venkatesh, and Avis Vidal. 2001. *Building Community Capacity*. New York: Aldine de Gruyter.

Chaskin, Robert J., and Mikael Karlström. 2012. "Beyond the Neighborhood Report: Policy Engagement and Systems Change in the New Communities Program." New York: MDRC.

Chen, Bin, and Elizabeth A. Graddy. 2010. "The Effectiveness of Nonprofit Lead-Organization Networks for Social Service Delivery." *Nonprofit Management & Leadership* 20(4):405–22.

Chicago Mayor's Office, CMAP, LISC Chicago, South East Chicago Commission, and Washington Park Consortium. 2014. "Green Healthy Neighborhoods." Chicago: Chicago Department of Planning and Development.

Chicago Mayor's Press Office. 2013. "Land Sale Would Enable Norfolk Southern Rail Yard Expansion." February 13. www.chicago.gov.

Chua, Roy Young Joo, Paul Ingram, and Michael W. Morris. 2008. "From the Head and the Heart: Locating Cognition—and Affect-Based Trust in Managers' Professional Networks." *Academy of Management Journal* 51(3):436–52.

Chuy for Congress. 2014. "About Chuy." http://jesuschuygarcia.com.

Clay, P. 1990. "Mainstreaming the Community Builders: The Challenge of Expanding Capacity of Non-profit Housing Development Organizations." Cambridge: Massachusetts Institute of Technology, Department of Urban Studies and Planning.

Clemens, Elisabeth S., and Doug Guthrie. 2010. *Politics and Partnerships: The Role of Voluntary Associations in America's Political Past and Present*. Chicago: University of Chicago Press.

CMAP. 2012. "GOTO 2040 Introduction." Chicago: Chicago Metropolitan Agency for Planning.

CMAP and HED. 2013. "GHN Large Lot Pilot Program." Chicago: Chicago Metropolitan Agency for Planning.

CNT. 2014. "Transit Deserts in Cook County." Chicago: Center for Neighborhood Technology.

Coleman, James S. 1974. *Power and the Structure of Society*. New York: Norton.

——. 1988. "Social Capital in the Creation of Human Capital." *American Journal of Sociology* 94:95–120.

Collins, Patricia Hill. 2000. *Black Feminist Thought: Knowledge, Consciousness, and the Politics of Empowerment*. 2nd ed. New York: Routledge.

Connell, Robert. 2011. "National People of Color Environmental Leadership Summit." In *Green Culture: An A-to-Z Guide*, edited by Kevin Wehr. Thousand Oaks, CA: Sage.

Cross, Rob, Andrew Parker, Laurence Prusak, and Stephan P. Borgatti. 2001. "Knowing What We Know: Supporting Knowledge Creation and Sharing in Social Networks." *Organizational Dynamics* 30(2):100–120.

Curran, Winifred, and Euan Hague. 2006. "The Pilsen Building Inventory Project." Chicago: DePaul University Department of Geography for the Pilsen Alliance.

Dávila, Arlene. 2004. "Empowered Culture? New York City's Empowerment Zone and the Selling of El Barrio." *Annals of the American Academy of Political and Social Science* 594:49–64.

Davis, Gerald F., and Henrich R. Greve. 1997. "Corporate Elite Networks and Governance Changes in the 1980s." *American Journal of Sociology* 103(1):1–37.

DeFilippis, James. 2001. "The Myth of Social Capital in Community Development." *Housing Policy Debate* 12(4):781–806.

De Genova, Nicholas. 2005. *Working the Boundaries: Race, Space, and "Illegality" in Mexican Chicago*. Durham, NC: Duke University Press.

Dekker, Paul, and Eric M. Uslaner, eds. 2003. *Social Capital and Participation in Everyday Life*. London: Routledge.

DelSesto, Matthew. 2015. "Cities, Gardening, and Urban Citizenship: Transforming Vacant Acres into Community Resources." *Cities and the Environment* 8(2). https://digitalcommons.lmu.edu/cate/vol8/iss2/3.

Dexter, Louis Anthony. 2006. *Elite and Specialized Interviewing*. Vol. 13. Colchester: European Consortium for Political Research.

DiMaggio, Paul J., and Walter W. Powell, eds. 1991. *The New Institutionalism in Organizational Analysis*. Chicago: University of Chicago Press.

Drake, St. Clair, and Horace R. Cayton. 1945. *Black Metropolis: A Study of Negro Life in a Northern City*. Chicago: University of Chicago Press.

Du Bois, W. E. B. 1903. *The Souls of Black Folk: Essays and Sketches*. Chicago: A. C. McClurg.

Duncan, Cynthia M. 2014. *Worlds Apart: Poverty and Politics in Rural America*. 2nd ed. New Haven, CT: Yale University Press.

Emejulu, Akwugo. 2011. "Re-theorizing Feminist Community Development: Towards a Radical Democratic Citizenship." *Community Development Journal* 46(3):378–90.

Enlace and LISC/Chicago. 2005. "Little Village: Capital of the Midwest." Chicago: LISC/Chicago.

Ennis, Gretchen, and Deborah West. 2012. "Using Social Network Analysis in Community Development Practice and Research: A Case Study." *Community Development Journal* 48(1):40–57.

EPA. 2008a. "PPA Exhibit 4: Administrative Settlement." U.S. Environmental Protection Agency, Region V.

———. 2008b. "PPA Exhibit 4: Administrative Settlement Agreement and Covenant Not to Sue City of Chicago or Chicago Park District." U.S. Environmental Protection Agency, Region V.

———. 2011. "Celotex: Background." U.S. Environmental Protection Agency.

———. 2014. "Celotex Superfund Site: Site Updates." U.S. Environmental Protection Agency.

Fainstein, Susan S. 2011. "Redevelopment Planning and Distributive Justice in the American Metropolis." In *Justice and the American Metropolis*, edited by Clarisa Rile Hayward and Todd Swanstrom. Minneapolis: University of Minnesota Press.

Ferguson, Ronald F., and Sara E. Stoutland. 1999. "Reconceiving the Community Development Field." In *Urban Problems and Community Development*, edited by Ronald F. Ferguson and William T. Dickens. Washington, DC: Brookings Institution Press.

Finkel, Ed. 2012. "NCP Turns 10." *LISC Chicago's New Communities Program*, March 14.

Fligstein, Neil. 2001. "Social Skill and the Theory of Fields." *Sociological Theory* 19(2):105–25.

Fraser, Nancy. 1990. "Rethinking the Public Sphere: A Contribution to the Critique of Actually Existing Democracy." *Social Text* 25/26:56–80.

Fukuyama, Francis. 1995. *Trust*. New York: Free Press.

Fung, Archon. 2004. *Empowered Participation*. Princeton, NJ: Princeton University Press.

Garrison, Andrew. 2007. *Third Ward, TX*. Houston: Welcome Home Productions.

Gibbs, Adrienne Samuels. 2015. "The Problem with 'Chiraq.'" *Chicago Magazine*, April 9.

Gilchrist, Alison, and Marilyn Taylor. 1997. "Community Networking: Developing Strength through Diversity." In *Contested Communities: Experiences, Struggles, Policies*, edited by Paul Hoggett. Bristol: Policy.

Giloth, Robert, Charles Orlebeke, James Tickell, and Patricia Wright. 1992. "Choices Ahead: CDCs and Real Estate Production in Chicago." Chicago: Nathalie P. Voorhees Center for Neighborhood and Community Improvement.

Gittell, Ross, and J. Phillip Thomson. 2001. "Making Social Capital Work: Social Capital and Community Economic Development." In *Social Capital and Poor Communities*, edited by Susan Saegert, J. Phillip Thompson, and Mark R. Warren, 115–32. New York: Russell Sage Foundation.

Gonzales, Teresa. 2017. "Two Sides of the Same Coin: The New Communities Program, Grassroots Organizations, and Leadership Development in Two Chicago Neighborhoods." *Journal of Urban Affairs* 39(8):1138–54.

Granovetter, Mark S. 1973. "The Strength of Weak Ties." *American Journal of Sociology* 78(6):1360–1380.

———. 1983. "The Strength of Weak Ties: A Network Theory Revisited." *Sociological Theory* 1:201–33.

Green, Gary Paul, and Anna Haines. 2012. *Asset Building & Community Development*. 3rd ed. Thousand Oaks, CA: Sage.

Greenberg, David, Nandita Verma, Keri-Nicole Dillman, and Robert J. Chaskin. 2010. "Creating a Platform for Sustained Neighborhood Improvement: Interim Findings from Chicago's New Communities Program." New York: MDRC.

Greenwood, Daphne T., and Richard P. F. Holt. 2010. *Local Economic Development in the 21st Century: Quality of Life and Sustainability*. Armonk, NY: M.E. Sharpe.

Greenwood, Royston, and C. R. Hinings. 2006. "Radical Organizational Change." In *Handbook of Organization Studies*, edited by Stewart R. Clegg, Cynthia Hardy, Walter R. Nord, and Thomas B. Lawrence. Thousand Oaks, CA: Sage.

Gregory, Stephen. 1999. *Black Corona: Race and the Politics of Place in an Urban Community*. Princeton, NJ: Princeton University Press.

Grimshaw, Lucy. 2011. "Community Work as Women's Work? The Gendering of English Neighborhood Partnerships." *Community Development Journal* 46(3):327–40.

Grossman, Ron. 2013. "Chicago Political History Rife with Nepotism, Aldermanic Dynasties." *Chicago Tribune*, July 31.

Guidotti-Hernández, Nicole M. 2017. "Affective Communities and Millennial Desires: Latinx, or Why My Computer Won't Recognize Latina/o." *Cultural Dynamics* 29(3):141–59.

Hardy, Cynthia, Nelson Phillips, and Thomas B. Lawrence. 1998. "Distinguishing Trust and Power in Interorganizational Relationships: Forms and Façades of Trust." In *Trust Within and Between Organizations*, edited by Christel Lane and Reinhard Bachmann. Oxford: Oxford University Press.

Hart, Chris, Kathryn Jones, and Manmohan Bains. 1997. "Do the People Want Power? The Social Responsibilities of Empowering Communities." In *Contested Communities: Experiences, Struggles, Policies*, edited by Paul Hoggett. Bristol: Policy.

Haus, Michael, and David Sweeting. 2006. "Local Democracy and Political Leadership: Drawing a Map." *Political Studies* 54:267–88.

Hilkevitch, Jon. 2014. "'Transit Deserts' Don't Serve Workers, Study Says." *Chicago Tribune*, August 3.

Hirsch, Arnold R. 2005. "Urban Renewal." In *The Electronic Encyclopedia of Chicago*. Chicago: Chicago Historical Society and Newberry Library. http://encyclopedia.chicagohistory.org.

Hoang, Kimberly K. 2015. *Dealing in Desire*. Oakland: University of California Press.

Huisman, Kimberly. 2008. "'Does This Mean You're Not Going to Come Visit Me Anymore?' An Inquiry into an Ethics of Reciprocity and Positionality in Feminist Ethnographic Research." *Sociological Inquiry* 78(3):372–96.

Hunter, Lori. 2000. "The Spatial Association between U.S. Immigrant Residential Concentration and Environmental Hazards." *International Migration Review* 34(2):460–88.

Isoke, Zenzele. 2013. *Urban Black Women and the Politics of Resistance*. New York: Palgrave Macmillan.

Jenkins, J. Craig. 1985. "Foundation Funding of Progressive Social Movements." In *The Grant Seekers Guide*, edited by Jill Shellow. Nyack, NY: Glenmeade.

Jiao, Junfeng, and Maxwell Dillivan. 2013. "Transit Deserts: The Gap between Demand and Supply." *Journal of Public Transportation* 16(3):23–39.

Keefe, Alex. 2013. "Pregnancy Tests? Pigeon Poo? What Chicago Aldermen Really Do." In *Curious City*. WBEZ 91.5.

Kelleher, Maureen. 2012. "Thinking through Evaluation." LISC Institute for Comprehensive Community Development. http://www.instituteccd.org.

Keyes, Langley C., Alex Schwartz, Avis C. Vidal, and Rachel G. Bratt. 1996. "Networks and Nonprofits: Opportunities and Challenges in an Era of Federal Devolution." *Housing Policy Debate* 7(2):201–23.

Kingsley, Thomas G., Joseph McNeely, and James O. Gibson. 1997. *Community Building: Coming of Age*. Washington, DC: Urban Institute.

Knox, Douglas. 2005. *Ward System*. Chicago: Chicago Historical Society.

Kretzmann, John P., and John L. McKnight. 1997. *Building Communities from the Inside Out: A Path towards Finding and Mobilizing a Community's Assets*. Skokie, IL: ACTA.

Kroeger, Frens. 2011. "Trusting Organizations: The Institutionalization of Trust in Interorganizational Relationships." *Organization* 19(6):743–63.

Kubisch, Anne C., Patricia Auspos, Prudence Brown, Robert J. Chaskin, Karen Fulbright-Anderson, and Ralph Hamilton. 2002. *Voices from the Field II: Reflections on Comprehensive Community Change*. Washington, DC: Aspen Institute.

Kubisch, Anne C., Prudence Brown, Robert J. Chaskin, M. Hirota, Mark L. Joseph, H. Richman, and M. Roberts. 1997. *Voices from the Field: Learning from Comprehensive Community Initiatives*. Washington, DC: Aspen Institute.

Kumar, Sanjay, and Stuart Corbridge. 2002. "Programmed to Fail? Development Projects and the Politics of Participation." *Journal of Development Studies* 39(2):73–103.

Lambright, Kristina T., Pamela A. Mischen, and Craig B. Laramee. 2010. "Building Trust in Public and Nonprofit Networks: Personal, Dyadic, and Third-Party Influences." *American Review of Public Administration* 40(1):64–82.

Lara, Jesus. 2018. *Latino Placemaking and Planning: Cultural Resilience and Strategies for Reurbanization*. Tucson: University of Arizona Press.

Leavitt, Jacqueline. 2006. "Linking Housing to CED with CBAs: The Case of the Figueroa Corridor Coalition for Economic Justice." In *Jobs and Economic Development in Minority Communities*, edited by Paul Ong and Anastasia Loukaitou-Sideris. Philadelphia: Temple University Press.

Lees, Loretta, Hyun Bang Shin, and Ernesto López-Morales. 2016. *Planetary Gentrification*. Malden, MA: Polity Press.

Lees, Loretta, Elvin K. Wyly, and Tom Slater. 2008. *Gentrification*. New York: Routledge.

LISC/Chicago. 2011. "About NCP."

Little Village Land, ed. 2010. "Little Village Community Design."

Logan, John R., and Harvey L. Molotch. 1987. *Urban Fortunes: The Political Economy of Place*. Berkeley: University of California Press.

Lowe, Jeffrey S. 2008. "Limitations of Community Development Partnerships: Cleveland Ohio and Neighborhood Progress Inc." *Cities* 25:37–44.

LVCDC. 2005. "Little Village: Capital of the Midwest." In *New Communities Program*, edited by LISC/Chicago. Chicago: Local Initiatives Support Corporation.

LVEJO. 2009. "USEPA Ignores Massive Contamination on the New Planned Park Site in Little Village." Little Village Land.

MacFound. 2012. "Grantee Profile—Local Initiatives Support Corporation." John D. and Catherine T. MacArthur Foundation.

Maher, Timothy. 1998. "Environmental Oppression: Who Is Targeted for Toxic Exposure?" *Journal of Black Studies* 28(3):357–67.

Malizia, Emil E., and Edward J. Feser. 1999. "Understanding Local Economic Development." New Brunswick, NJ: Center for Urban Policy Research.

Mansbridge, Jane. 1990. "Feminism and Democracy." *American Prospect* 1(1). https://prospect.org.

———. 1996. "Using Power/Fighting Power: The Polity." In *Democracy and Difference: Contesting the Boundaries of the Political*, edited by Seyla Benhabib. Princeton, NJ: Princeton University Press.

Mansuri, Ghazala, and Vijayendra Rao. 2004. "Community-Based and -Driven Development: A Critical Review." *World Bank Research Observer* 19(1):1–39.

Marwell, Nicole. 2004. "Privatizing the Welfare State: Nonprofit Community-Based Organizations as Political Actors." *American Sociological Review* 69(2):26.

———. 2007. *Bargaining for Brooklyn: Community Organizations in the Entrepreneurial City*. Chicago: University of Chicago Press.

Massey, Douglas S. 1996. "The Age of Extremes: Concentrated Affluence and Poverty in the Twenty-First Century." *Demography* 33:395–412.

Mayer, Neil, and Jennifer L. Blake. 1984. *Keys to the Growth of Neighborhood Development Corporations*. Washington, DC: Urban Institute.

McAllister, Daniel J. 1995. "Affect- and Cognition-Based Trust as Foundations for Interpersonal Cooperation in Organizations." *Academy of Management Journal* 38(1):24–59.

McCarron, John. 2011. "Growing Green Healthy Neighborhoods." New Communities Program.

McQuarrie, Michael. 2010. "Nonprofits and the Reconstruction of Urban Governance: Housing Production and Community Development in Cleveland, 1975–2005." In *Politics and Partnerships: The Role of Voluntary Associations in America's Political Past and Present*, edited by Elisabeth S. Clemens and Doug Guthrie. Chicago: University of Chicago Press.

———. 2013. "No Contest: Participatory Technologies and the Transformation of Urban Authority." *Public Culture* 25(1):143–75.

Melucci, Alberto. 1996. *Challenging Codes: Collective Action in the Information Age*. Cambridge: Cambridge University Press.

Merton, Robert K. 1973. "The Normative Structure of Science." In *The Sociology of Science*, 267–78. Chicago: University of Chicago Press.

MetroPulse. 2017. "Community Data Snapshot: Englewood." Chicago: Chicago Metropolitan Agency for Planning.

Minkoff, Debra C. 1999. "Bending with the Wind: Strategic Change and Adaptation by Women's and Racial Minority Organizations." *American Journal of Sociology* 104(6):1666–1703.

Mitchell, Chip. 2011. "Settlement Could Lead to Big Park for Mexican Neighborhood." WBEZ 91.5.

Molotch, Harvey L. 1976. "The City as a Growth Machine: Toward a Political Economy of Place." *American Journal of Sociology* 82(2):309–32.

Morrison, Toni. 2003. "The Truest Eye." *O, The Oprah Magazine*, November.

Moser, Whet. 2011. "The Housing Crisis on Chicago's South Side." *Chicago Magazine*, June 24.

NCP. 2005. "Little Village Rolls Out Quality of Life Plan." New Communities Program.

———. 2006. "Community Investment Portfolio: 14 Catalytic Projects." Chicago: Local Initiatives Support Corporation.

O'Connor, Alice. 1999. "Swimming Against the Tide: A Brief History of Federal Policy in Poor Communities." In *Urban Problems and Community Development*, edited by Ronald F. Ferguson and William T. Dickens. Washington, DC: Brookings Institution Press.

Olivo, Antonio. 2006. "Railyard Rattles Neighbors." *Chicago Tribune*, April 10.

Olivo, Antonio, William Mullen, and Dahleen Glanton. 2011. "Vacant Homes Keep Englewood in Downward Spiral." *Chicago Tribune*, June 24.

O'Reilly, Charles A., III. 1982. "Variations in Decision Makers' Use of Information Sources: The Impact of Quality and Accessibility of Information." *Academy of Management Journal* 25(4):756–71.

Pastor, Manuel, Chris Benner, and Matha Matsuoka. 2009. *This Could Be the Start of Something Big: How Social Movements for Regional Equity Are Reshaping Metropolitan America*. Ithaca, NY: Cornell University Press.

Pelaez Lopez, Alan. 2018. "The X in Latinx Is a Wound, Not a Trend." *Color Bloq*. www .colorbloq.org.

Pellow, David Naguib. 2002. *Garbage Wars: The Struggle for Environmental Justice in Chicago*. Cambridge, MA: MIT Press.

Perez, Gina. 2004. *The Near Northwest Side Story*. Berkeley: University of California Press.

Pfeffer, Jeffrey, and Gerald R. Salancik. [1978] 2003. *The External Control of Organizations: A Resource Dependence Perspective*. Stanford, CA: Stanford Business Books.

Pharr, Suzanne. 1996. *In the Time of the Right: Reflections on Liberation*. Inverness, CA: Chardon Press.

Polletta, Francesca. 2002. *Freedom in an Endless Meeting*. Chicago: University of Chicago Press.

Porter, Michael E. 1995. "New Strategies for Inner-City Economic Development." *EDQ* 11(1).

Portes, Alejandro, and Julia Sensenbrenner. 1993. "Embeddedness and Immigration: Notes on the Social Determinants of Economic Action." *American Journal of Sociology* 98(6):1320–50.

Portes, Alejandro, and Alex Stepick. 1993. *City on the Edge: The Transformation of Miami*. Berkeley: University of California Press.

Powell, Walter W. 2007. "The New Institutionalism." In *The International Encyclopedia of Organization Studies*, edited by Stewart R. Clegg and James R. Bailey. Thousand Oaks, CA: Sage.

Putnam, Robert D. 1994. "Social Capital and Public Affairs." *Bulletin of the American Academy of Arts and Sciences* 47(8):5–19.

———. 1995. "Bowling Alone: America's Declining Social Capital." *Journal of Democracy* 6(1):65–78.

Pyles, Loretta. 2014. *Progressive Community Organizing: Reflective Practice in a Globalizing World.* 2nd ed. New York: Routledge.

Rankin, Bruce, and James Quane. 2000. "Neighborhood Poverty and Social Isolation of Inner-City African-American Families." *Social Forces* 79(1):139–64.

Rankin, Sarah. 2015. "Building Sustainable Communities: Integrated Services and Improved Financial Outcomes for Low-Income Households." Local Initiatives Support Corporation.

Rezin, Ashlee. 2013. "EPA Makes Commitment to Clean Up Pollution in Pilsen, Little Village." *Progress Illinois.*

Rich, Lauren. 2013. "Technical Assistance to Local Initiatives Support Corporation of Chicago (LISC) 'Testing the Model' Sites." Chapin Hall at the University of Chicago.

Rios, Michael, and Leonardo Vazquez, eds. 2012. *Diálogos: Placemaking in Latino Communities.* Oxford: Taylor & Francis.

Rios, Victor. 2011. *Punished: Policing the Lives of Black and Latino Boys.* New York: New York University Press.

———. 2015. "Help for Kids the Education System Ignores." In *TED Talks Live,* November 16.

Rodriguez, Cheryl. 1998. "Activist Stories: Culture and Continuity in Black Women's Narratives of Grassroots Community Work." *Frontiers: A Journal of Women Studies* 19(2):94–112.

Rodriguez, Juana María. 2014. *Sexual Futures, Queer Gestures, and Other Latina Longings.* New York: New York University Press.

Ross, Catherine E., John Mirowsky, and Shana Pribesh. 2001. "Powerlessness and the Amplification of Threat: Disadvantage, Disorder, and Mistrust." *American Sociological Review* 66(4):568–91.

Rotter, Julian B. 1980. "Interpersonal Trust, Trustworthiness, and Gullibility." *American Psychologist* 35:1–7.

Rousseau, Denise M., Sim B. Sitkin, Ronald S. Burt, and Colin Camerer. 1998. "Not So Different after All: A Cross-Discipline View of Trust." *Academy of Management Journal* 23(3):393–404.

Rusk, David. 1999. *Inside Game Outside Game: Winning Strategies for Saving Urban America.* Washington, DC: Brookings Institution Press.

Salamon, Lester M. 1987. "Of Market Failure, Voluntary Failure, and Third-Party Government: Toward a Theory of Government-Nonprofit Relations in the Modern Welfare State." In *Shifting the Debate: Public/Private Sector Relations in the Modern Welfare State,* edited by Susan A. Ostrander and Stuart Langton. New Brunswick, NJ: Transaction Books.

———. 1995. *Partners in Public Service: Government-Nonprofit Relations in the Modern Welfare State.* New Brunswick, NJ: Transaction Books.

Sampson, Robert. 2012. *Great American City: Chicago and the Enduring Neighborhood Effect*. Chicago: University of Chicago Press.

Sampson, Robert, and Stephen W. Raudenbush. 1999. "Systemic Social Observation of Public Spaces: A New Look at Disorder in Urban Neighborhoods." *American Journal of Sociology* 105(3):603–51.

Sánchez-Jankowski, Martín. 2008. *Cracks in the Pavement: Social Change and Resilience in Poor Neighborhoods*. Berkeley: University of California Press.

Sander, Thomas H., and Robert D. Putnam. 2010. "Still Bowling Alone? The Post-9/11 Split." *Journal of Democracy* 21(1):9–16.

Scott, W. Richard. 2000. *Institutions and Organizations*. 2nd ed. Thousand Oaks, CA: Sage.

SEI. 2013. "Current Project: Getting Englewood a Fair Deal on the Expansion of the Norfolk Southern Rail Yard." Chicago: Sustainable Englewood Initiatives.

Seyfang, Gill, and Noel Longhurst. 2013. "Growing Green Money? Mapping Community Currencies for Sustainable Development." *Ecological Economics* 86:65–77.

Sfondeles, Tina. 2014. "City Wants to Offer Vacant Englewood Lots for a Dollar." *Chicago Sun-Times*, March 19.

Shipley, Robert. 2000. "The Origin and Development of Vision and Visioning in Planning." *International Planning Studies* 5(2):225–36.

Silverman, Robert Mark. 2005. "Caught in the Middle: Community Development Corporations (CDCs) and the Conflict between Grassroots and Instrumental Forms of Citizen Participation." *Community Development* 36(2):35–51.

Simon, William H. 2001. *The Community Economic Development Movement: Law, Business, and the New Social Policy*. Durham, NC: Duke University Press.

Skocpol, Theda. 2003. *Diminished Democracy: From Membership to Management in American Civic Life*. Norman: University of Oklahoma Press.

Slife, Erika. 2010. "Little Village Residents Pine for Park on Vacant Land." *Chicago Tribune*, December 6.

Small, Mario. 2004. *Villa Victoria: The Transformation of Social Capital in a Boston Barrio*. Chicago: University of Chicago Press.

———. 2009. *Unanticipated Gains: Origins of Network Inequality in Everyday Life*. Oxford: Oxford University Press.

———. 2013. "Weak Ties and the Core Discussion Network: Why People Regularly Discuss Important Matters with Unimportant Alters." *Social Networks* 35:470–83.

———. 2015. "De-exoticizing Ghetto Poverty: On the Ethics of Representation in Urban Ethnography." *City & Community* 14(4):352–58.

Smith, Neil. 1996. *The New Urban Frontier: Gentrification and the Revanchist City*. London: Routledge.

Smith, Neil, and Peter Williams, eds. 1986. *Gentrification of the City*. Boston: Allen & Unwin.

Smith, Sandra Susan. 2007. *Lone Pursuit: Distrust and Defensive Individualism among the Black Poor*. New York: Russell Sage Foundation.

Spielman, Fran. 2013a. "Expansion of TIFs OKd for Norfolk Southern Rail Yard in Englewood." *Chicago Sun-Times*, September 19.

———. 2013b. "Mayor's 'Strategic Vision' for Seven Neighborhoods." *Chicago Sun-Times*, March 16.

Squires, Gregory D., Larry Bennett, Kathleen McCourt, and Philip Nyden, eds. 1987. *Chicago: Race, Class, and the Response to Urban Decline*. Philadelphia: Temple University Press.

Stoecker, Randy. 1997. "The CDC Model of Urban Redevelopment: A Critique and an Alternative." *Journal of Urban Affairs* 19(1):1–22.

Stone, Clarence, Kathryn Doherty, Cheryl Jones, and Timothy Ross. 1999. "Schools and Disadvantaged Neighborhoods: The Community Development Challenge." In *Urban Problems and Community Development*, edited by Ronald F. Ferguson and William T. Dickens. Washington, DC: Brookings Institution Press.

Stoutland, Sara E. 1999. "Community Development Corporations: Mission, Strategy, and Accomplishments." In *Urban Problems and Community Development*, edited by Ronald F. Ferguson and William T. Dickens. Washington, DC: Brookings Institution Press.

Suppelsa, Mark. 2013. "'It's Englewood': 12 Hours in One of Chicago's Most Dangerous Neighborhoods." WGNTV, August 25.

Taylor, D. Garth, and Sylvia Puente. 2004. "Immigration, Gentrification and Chicago Race/Ethnic Relations in the New Global Era." Paper presented at the Changing Face of Metropolitan Chicago Conference on Chicago Research and Public Policy, Chicago, May 12–13.

Taylor, Dorceta E. 2014. *Toxic Communities: Environmental Racism, Industrial Pollution, and Residential Mobility*. New York: New York University Press.

Taylor, Marilyn. 2000. "Communities in the Lead: Power, Organisational Capacity, and Social Capital." *Urban Studies* 37(5–6):1019–35.

Teamwork Englewood and LISC/Chicago. 2005. "Englewood: Making a Difference." Chicago: LISC/Chicago.

Temkin, Kenneth, and William Rohe. 1998. "Social Capital and Neighborhood Stability: An Empirical Investigation." *Housing Policy Debate* 9(1):61–88.

Tessum, Christopher W., Joshua S. Apte, Andrew L. Goodkind, Nicholas Z. Muller, Kimberley A. Mullins, David A. Paolella, Stephen Polasky, Nathaniel P. Springer, Sumil K. Thakrar, Julian D. Marshall, and Jason D. Hill. 2019. "Inequity in Consumption of Goods and Services Adds to Racial-Ethnic Disparities in Air Pollution Exposure." *Proceedings of the National Academy of Sciences USA* 116(13):6001–6.

Trainor, Audrey, and Kate Ahlgren Bouchard. 2012. "Exploring and Developing Reciprocity in Research Design." *International Journal of Qualitative Studies in Education* 26(8):986–1003.

Trujillo-Pagán, Nicole. 2018. "Crossed Out by LatinX: Gender Neutrality and Gender-blind Sexism." *Latino Studies* 16(3):396–406.

Tsao, Fred. 2014. "Illinois' Undocumented Immigrant Population: A Summary of Recent Research by Rob Paral and Associates." Chicago: Illinois Coalition for Immigrant and Refugee Rights; Rob Paral and Associates.

Tsasis, Peter. 2009. "The Social Processes of Interorganizational Collaboration and Conflict in Nonprofit Organizations." *Nonprofit Management & Leadership* 20(1):5–21.

Vargas, Deborah R. 2014. "Ruminations on *Lo Sucio* as a Latino Queer Analytic." *American Quarterly* 66(3):715–26.

Vargas, Robert. 2016. *Wounded City: Violent Turf Wars in a Chicago Barrio*. New York: Oxford University Press.

Vidal, Avis. 1992. *Rebuilding Communities: A National Study of Urban Community Development Corporations*. New York: New School for Social Research, Community Development Research Center, Graduate School of Management and Urban Policy.

Voutira, Eftihia, and Barbara E. Harrell-Bond. 1995. "In Search of the Locus of Trust: The Social World of the Refugee Camp." In *Mistrusting Refugees*, edited by E. Valentine Daniel and John Chr. Knudsen. Berkeley: University of California Press.

Wacquant, Loïc. 2008. "Relocating Gentrification: The Working Class, Science and the State in Recent Urban Research." *International Journal of Urban and Regional Research* 32(1):198–205.

Walker, Chris, Sarah Rankin, and Francisca Winston. 2010. "New Approaches to Comprehensive Neighborhood Change: Replicating and Adapting LISC's Building Sustainable Communities Program." Chicago: Local Initiatives Support Corporation.

Warren, Mark E., ed. 1999. *Democracy and Trust*. Cambridge: Cambridge University Press.

Weir, Margaret. 1999. "Power, Money, and Politics in Community Development." In *Urban Problems and Community Development*, edited by Ronald F. Ferguson and William T. Dickens. Washington, DC: Brookings Institution Press.

Wherry, Frederick F. 2011. *The Philadelphia Barrio: The Arts, Branding, and Neighborhood Transformation*. Chicago: University of Chicago Press.

Wilson, William Julius. 1987. *The Truly Disadvantaged: The Inner City, the Underclass, and Public Policy*. Chicago: University of Chicago Press.

Wolman, Harold, and David Spitzley. 1996. "The Politics of Local Economic Development." *Economic Development Quarterly* 10(2):115–50.

Worthy, Sheri Lokken, Crystal Tyler-Mackey, Patricia Hyjer Dyk, Pamela A. Monroe, and Rachel Welborn. 2016. "Turning the Tide on Poverty: Perceptions of Leaders and Leadership in Economically Distressed Communities." *Community Development* 47(3):322–40.

Zielenbach, Sean. 2000. *The Art of Revitalization: Improving Conditions in Distressed Inner-City Neighborhoods*. New York: Garland.

Zolin, Roxanne, and Pamela J. Hinds. 2004. "Trust in Context: The Development of Interpersonal Trust in Geographically Distributed Work." In *Trust and Distrust in Organizations: Dilemmas and Approaches*, edited by Roderick M. Kramer and Karen S. Cook. New York: Russell Sage Foundation.

INDEX

Page numbers in *italics* indicate figures, tables, and photos.

ABOUT THE AUTHOR

A native of Mexican Chicago, TERESA IRENE GONZALES is Assistant Professor of Sociology at the University of Massachusetts, Lowell. She received her doctorate and master's degrees from the University of California, Berkeley in sociology, and her bachelor's degree from Smith College in Latin American & Latina/o studies with a focus on literature and history. She firmly believes in the capacity of sociology to redress social injustices and inequalities. As a feminist, and a woman of color urbanist, Gonzales is rooted in community-engaged pedagogy and scholarship and strives toward a practice of reciprocity in research. Her work has appeared in the *Journal of Urban Affairs* and *Social Problems*, in edited volumes, and on *Academic Minute*. She has received both internal and extramural funding/support, notably from the Woodrow Wilson Foundation, the SSRC-Mellon Mays Graduate Initiatives Program, the Community Development Society, and the UC Berkeley Center for Latino Policy Research.

Printed in the USA
CPSIA information can be obtained
at www.ICGtesting.com
LVHW050911270124
769821LV00021B/200